Tunisia 1943

COMBAT

US Soldier

VERSUS

Afrikakorps Soldier

David Campbell

Illustrated by Steve Noon

OSPREY PUBLISHING
Bloomsbury Publishing Plc
PO Box 883, Oxford, OX1 9PL, UK
1385 Broadway, 5th Floor, New York, NY 10018, USA
E-mail: info@ospreypublishing.com
www.ospreypublishing.com

OSPREY is a trademark of Osprey Publishing Ltd

First published in Great Britain in 2019

A catalog record for this book is available from the British Library.

ISBN: PB 9781472828163; eBook 9781472828170;
ePDF 9781472828187; XML 9781472828194

19 20 21 22 23   10 9 8 7 6 5 4 3 2 1

Maps by bounford.com
Index by Rob Munro
Typeset by PDQ Digital Media Solutions, Bungay, UK
Printed in China through World Print Ltd.
Osprey Publishing supports the Woodland Trust, the UK's leading
woodland conservation charity.

To find out more about our authors and books visit
www.ospreypublishing.com. Here you will find extracts, author
interviews, details of forthcoming events and the option to sign up for
our newsletter.

Comparative ranks

US Army	Heer
General of the Army	*Generalfeldmarschall*
General	*Generaloberst*
Lieutenant General	*General der Infanterie*
Major General	*Generalleutnant*
Brigadier General	*Generalmajor*
Colonel	*Oberst*
Lieutenant Colonel	*Oberstleutnant*
Major	*Major*
Captain	*Hauptmann*
1st Lieutenant	*Oberleutnant*
2nd Lieutenant	*Leutnant*
Sergeant Major	*Stabsfeldwebel*
Master Sergeant	*Oberfeldwebel*
Staff Sergeant	*Feldwebel*
Sergeant	*Unterfeldwebel*
Corporal	*Unteroffizier*
n/a	*Obergefreiter*
Lance Corporal	*Gefreiter*
Private First Class	*Obergrenadier/Oberschütze*
Private	*Grenadier/Schütze*

Dedication

For Crichton Campbell: a talented failure, like the rest of us.

Acknowledgments

Thanks are due to Graham Campbell, who has taken on the burden
of Geoff Banks and his many, many concomitant needs; to David
Greentree for his encouragement and good advice, most of which was
naturally ignored; and to Nick Reynolds for his necessarily deep reserves
of patience.

Editor's note

In both the US and German armies, companies and artillery batteries
were given identifying numbers or letters that continued through
the sequence of battalions (or *Abteilungen* – normally battalion-sized
subunits) within a regiment. In the case of US units, letters are used
for companies, and Arabic numerals for battalions; A/168th Infantry
refers to Company A, 168th Infantry Regiment, which served in
the 1st Battalion, while 1/168th Infantry refers to the 1st Battalion,
168th Infantry Regiment. In the case of German units, Arabic numerals
are used for companies, and Roman numerals for battalions/*Abteilungen*
within a regiment; 1./PzArtRgt 90 refers to 1. Batterie, Panzer-Artillerie-
Regiment 90, which served in I. Abteilung, while I./PzArtRgt 90
indicates I. Abteilung, Panzer-Artillerie-Regiment 90.

Artist's note

Readers may care to note that the original paintings from which the
color plates in this book were prepared are available for private sale. All
reproduction copyright whatsoever is retained by the publishers. All
inquiries should be addressed to:

www.steve-noon.co.uk

The publishers regret that they can enter into no correspondence upon
this matter.

Glossary

AFAB	armored field artillery battalion
AufklAbt	*Aufklärungs-Abteilung* (reconnaissance battalion)
Bataillon	battalion
FAB	field artillery battalion
FAR	field artillery regiment
FlaK	*Fliegerabwehrkanone* (antiaircraft gun)
Kompanie	company
Kradschützen	motorcycle riflemen
mot.	*motorisiert* (motorized)
Nachrichten	signals
PzArtRgt	*Panzer-Artillerie-Regiment* (armored artillery regiment)
PzGrenRgt	*Panzergrenadier-Regiment* (armored infantry regiment)
PzJgAbt	*Panzerjäger-Abteilung* (antitank battalion)
PzPiBtl	*Panzer-Pionier-Bataillon* (armored pioneer battalion)
PzRgt	*Panzer-Regiment* (tank regiment)
Sonderverband	special unit
sPzAbt	*schwere Panzer-Abteilung* (heavy tank battalion)
TDB	tank destroyer battalion
zbV	*zur besonderen Verwendung* (special-purpose)
Zug	platoon

CONTENTS

Introduction

At the beginning of 1943 the German Army in North Africa was in a precarious position. Along with its Italian allies it occupied the east of Tunisia, running from Bizerte in the north down to Mareth in the south, buttoned up by two Allied armies slowly closing in from opposite ends of the country. Generalfeldmarschall Erwin Rommel's Deutsch-Italienische Panzerarmee (comprised of the Deutsches Afrikakorps – DAK – and the Italian XX Corps and XXI Corps) had been decisively beaten in the Western Desert, its long retreat to the Tunisian border securing it a temporary reprieve as General Sir Bernard L. Montgomery's pursuing Eighth Army overextended its supply lines in pursuit. In the north the Allied landings of Operation *Torch* at Oran

Three American soldiers pose with the barrel, bipod, and baseplate of their 81mm M1 mortar in North Africa, 1943. Mortars proved to be particularly important weapons in the broken and mountainous terrain of Tunisia; each infantry battalion's heavy-weapons company had one mortar platoon of six M1s (54 to a division); the mortar and mount (baseplate and bipod) weighed 136lb and fired the M3 high-explosive antipersonnel shell (6.92lb, range 100–3,290yd), the M56 antimatériel shell (10.62lb, range 300–2,560yd), and the M57 chemical (FS "chemical smoke" or White Phosphorus) shell (11.86lb, range 300–2,465yd). (Eliot Elisofon/The LIFE Premium Collection/Getty Images)

A quartet of German prisoners of war taken during an Allied assault on German positions near Sened, March 2, 1943. The man on the far left wears a *Verwundetenabzeichen* (Wound Badge) in black, indicating that he has been injured at least once in combat (the badge was also available in silver for those wounded three times and gold for those wounded five or more times). Note that although the men wear the older-pattern M1940 tropical tunics, none appears to sport the "Afrikakorps" armband, even though, having been captured at Sened in the south of the country, they would almost certainly have come from a veteran DAK unit. Though entitled to wear the armband after two months of service in theater, many soldiers kept it for formal occasions or when on leave. (Eliot Elisofon/The LIFE Picture Collection/Getty Images)

in Algeria in November 1942 had threatened Axis control of Tunis, the most important logistical center remaining to the German and Italian forces in North Africa, but a quick Axis response demonstrated by the deployment of Generaloberst Hans-Jürgen von Arnim's new 5. Panzerarmee had stabilized the situation. Even so, Lieutenant-General Sir Kenneth A.N. Anderson's First Army (comprised of the British V Corps and IX Corps, the French 19e Corps d'Armée, and the US II Corps) had advanced to Tunisia's Eastern Dorsal mountain range that ran down the length of central Tunisia, though it lacked the strength to inflict a decisive defeat upon the Axis forces that opposed it.

For the Germans, a stalemate in the Eastern Dorsal or along the Mareth Line in the south was untenable – the more time that passed, the stronger the First and Eighth armies would become, while in that same period of time attritional Axis losses would continue and the supply situation, already dire, would only get worse; prevarication was just a way for the Axis to lose the battle more slowly. Operationally speaking, the main Axis fear was of an Allied drive from the Eastern Dorsal toward the coastal towns of Sfax or Sousse on the central Tunisian coast, which if successful would cut the country in two and sever the link between 5. Panzerarmee and the DAK, allowing each to be defeated in detail.

This strategic situation was complicated – for both sides – by unwieldy chains of command. For the Axis forces Rommel and Arnim retained their separate commands, despite Rommel outranking his fellow officer; Generalfeldmarschall Albert Kesselring, Oberbefehlshaber Süd beim italienischen Oberkommando (Commander-in-Chief South at the Italian High Command) was their direct superior, but operational control resided with the Comando Supremo, the Italian military High Command in Rome, in overall charge of the North African theater. Rommel and Arnim had very different styles of leadership, and more than once Kesselring found himself managing their competing personalities as much as their opposing views of how best to prosecute the campaign against the British and American forces arrayed against them. For the Allies operational control of First Army, a blend of three quite different international military organizations, proved

MAP KEY

By the end of January 1943 the campaign in Tunisia had reached something of an impasse. In the south General Bernard L. Montgomery's Eighth Army was consolidating in preparation for a major assault on the heavily defended Mareth Line, held by Generalfeldmarschall Erwin Rommel's Deutsch-Italienische Panzerarmee. In the north 5. Panzerarmee dominated the area around Bizerte and Tunis, the latter being the strategically vital port through which Generalfeldmarschall Albert Kesselring and the Comando Supremo supplied nearly all the Panzers, replacements, rations, and ammunition that kept their forces fighting. Lieutenant-General Sir Kenneth A.N. Anderson's First Army, a combination of British, French, and American units, had tried to march on Tunis after the Allied landings of Operation *Torch* at Oran in Algeria in November 1942, but had been beaten to the punch by the Germans. Now Anderson's forces were deployed in a line from the Mediterranean coast moving south, down along the Eastern Dorsal mountain range until it anchored on the northern banks of the large impassable salt lake, Chott el Djerid.

Responsibility for their defense fell mainly to Major General Lloyd R. Fredendall's II Corps: the 1st Armored Division had been broken up into four combat commands that were mostly too far away from one another to offer mutual support, while the infantry divisions – the 1st and 34th – were in an even worse predicament, their battalions and regiments scattered all along the main line of defense, often serving with French or British units that further complicated matters of communication and supply. The Eastern Dorsal was an effective impediment to an attacker or defender and so domination of its passes, the most important of which was Faïd, was essential for the conduct of any serious operation. Thus it was that when the Deutsches Afrikakorps' 21. Panzer-Division stormed the pass at the end of January 1943, taking it from a few hundred French troops poorly supported by their American allies, an important factor in the control of south-central Tunisia flipped from the Americans to the Germans. Rommel now had the perfect gateway for a strike right into the heart of the disorganized and thinly spread II Corps.

challenging, with gaps between the capabilities and communications of its four corps leading to strategic miscalculations and avoidable mistakes.

The US II Corps, under the command of Major General Lloyd R. Fredendall, played a crucial role in the establishment and defense of the Allied line along the Eastern Dorsal, the probable jumping-off point for any decisive Allied assault and also the most likely target for Axis spoiling attacks or even major offensives. Despite the impressive strength of the American formation, the amount of ground it was responsible for defending was beyond what it could reasonably manage, even with the support of some poorly equipped French units. In addition, II Corps' major elements – the 1st and 34th Infantry divisions and the 1st Armored Division – did not deploy as coherent forces, their regiments and combat commands being separated from their parent divisions and detailed off to different parts of the line on a seemingly ad hoc basis.

The shape of the coming battle would be determined by who struck first, and it was the Germans, using the hard-won experience that came from years of campaigning coupled with a very real appreciation of the precariousness of their strategic situation, who seized the initiative. Along the Mareth Line the best that could be hoped for was a series of delaying actions that would disrupt the advance of Montgomery's Eighth Army, while the northern flank was held by two British corps supported by sea and air power, but the south-central zone was thinly defended by the mostly untried men of II Corps. Skirmishes with American forces near Sened and some of the passes through the Eastern Dorsal mountains had exposed deficiencies in US tactics, and perhaps also in the fighting capabilities of the men themselves. For Rommel these were shortcomings that were ripe for exploitation.

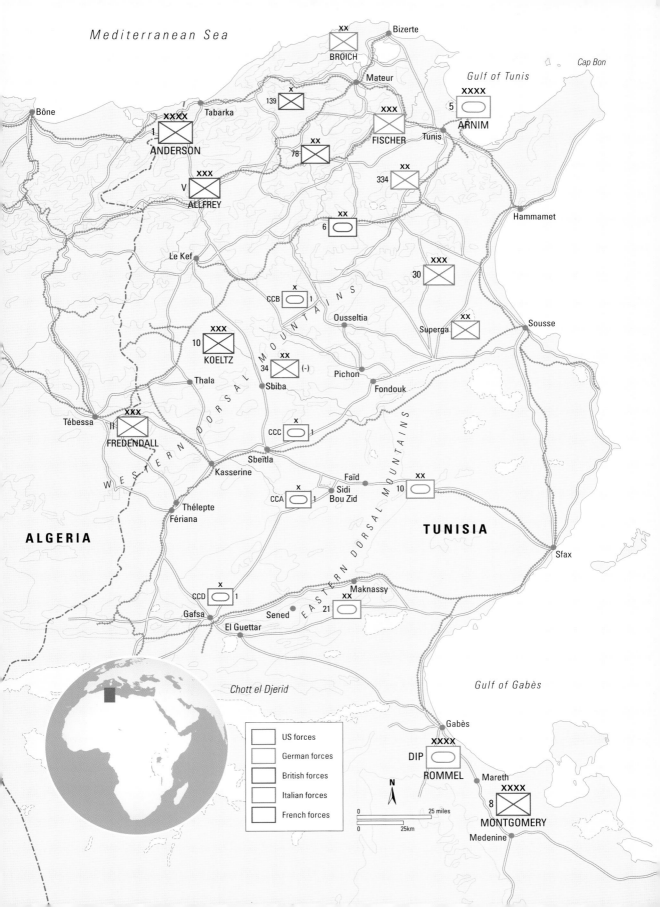

Mediterranean Sea

Bône

Bizerte

Mateur

Cap Bon

Gulf of Tunis

XX
BROICH

XXXX
5
ARNIM

Tabarka

x
139

XXX
FISCHER

Tunis

XXXX
1
ANDERSON

XX
78

XX
334

Hammamet

XXX
V
ALLFREY

XX
6

XXX
30

Le Kef

CCB x
1

Ousseltia

XX
Superga

Sousse

XXX
10
KOELTZ

WESTERN DORSAL MOUNTAINS

XX
34 (-)

Pichon

Fondouk

Thala

Sbiba

Tébessa

XXX
II
FREDENDALL

CCC x
1

Sbeïtla

EASTERN DORSAL MOUNTAINS

Kasserine

Faïd

XX
10

Sfax

CCA x
1

Sidi
Bou Zid

Thélepte
Fériana

TUNISIA

ALGERIA

CCD x
1

Maknassy

XX
21

Gafsa

Sened

El Guettar

Chott el Djerid

Gulf of Gabès

Gabès

XXXX
DIP
ROMMEL

Mareth

XXXX
8
MONTGOMERY

Medenine

	US forces
	German forces
	British forces
	Italian forces
	French forces

N

0   25 miles
0   25km

The Opposing Sides

ORIGINS AND ORGANIZATION

American

The 1st Infantry Division (Major General Terry de la Mesa Allen) won its reputation in World War I, during which, being the first US division organized for and fielded in that conflict, it was an integral part of the American Expeditionary Forces and took part in numerous battles, winning many plaudits for its performance. The end of the war saw the division's return to the United States where it was one of the nine regular infantry divisions kept on the Army's much-diminished peacetime establishment. The prospect of another war saw the division in the vanguard of the Army's push for reorganization and expansion, being the first unit to convert to the new "triangular" formation, but also seeing many of its regular service officers and men drafted away to serve as cadres for the raising of new divisions (though as it was likely to be one of the first divisions sent overseas this drain on its personnel was not as pronounced as it was for some other outfits). Dispatched to Europe in July–August 1942, it would form part of the assault force then being assembled for Operation *Torch*, the invasion of North Africa.

The 34th Infantry Division (Major General Charles W. Ryder) was a National Guard unit that drew its manpower from Iowa, Minnesota, North Dakota, and South Dakota; it also had been previously marked for service in World War I, but it only reached Europe in October 1918 and was never detailed to the front. One of 18 National Guard divisions activated as part of the Army's expansion program, the 34th Infantry Division was federalized (i.e. taken into Federal service as opposed to remaining under the jurisdiction of local state governors) on February 10, 1941, undergoing conversion to a "triangular" formation and conducting its basic training at Camp Claiborne, and taking part in the Louisiana Maneuvers later in 1941. It was the first

GIs move past the shattered remnants of a German tank during the successful Allied counterattack through the Kasserine Pass, late February 1943. The men who made up both regular Army and National Guard divisions were mostly draftees by the time they were deployed overseas (Congress had authorized the establishment of a national draft on September 16, 1940). The regular Army divisions had been drained of experienced men to form cadres upon which the 18 National Guard divisions being raised throughout 1940–41 could be built (Sayen 2006: 7–8). (© CORBIS/Corbis via Getty Images)

US division to be sent overseas, its various units shipping out for Northern Ireland between January 15 and May 13, 1942.

The Louisiana and Carolina maneuvers, held in the summer and fall of 1941, were the first large-scale test of the new Army, and showed that there were serious deficiencies in senior leadership, tactics, and infantry training. Action was taken to correct the problems, including remedial training programs for all infantry units at battalion level and below, though the process of ongoing recruitment and expansion (and in the case of the 1st and 34th Infantry divisions, deployment overseas) interfered with such attempts. Despite such growing pains, the one armored and two infantry divisions that would serve in Tunisia were well-equipped with modern weapons, and manned by soldiers who, though they might lack experience, had the potential to evolve into a fine fighting force.

American troops take a break in the run-up to the Allied attack on Axis positions at Sened, February 1, 1943. In the wake of World War I the US Army spent a considerable amount of time considering the best organizational structure for its infantry divisions, which had been using the "square" formation since 1914 (the term "square" referred to the fact that the divisions all had four infantry regiments in two brigades), finally settling on the "triangular" structure in December 1938 (initially for regular divisions – National Guard divisions did not make the move to a triangular structure until 1941–42). The reduction in the number of regiments in a division allowed the raising of five new divisions (4–8) by August 1940. The surplus regiments from the National Guard divisional conversions (which occurred through late 1941 and early 1942) were not used to raise new units, instead being mostly parceled out to garrison and rear-area security duties (Sayen 2006: 7–8). (Eliot Elisofon/The LIFE Picture Collection/Getty Images)

The gunner carries an M1918A2 Browning Automatic Rifle (BAR), but has discarded the awkward, cumbersome, and badly designed bipod that was normally attached to the flash hider. Originally capable of single shots or fully automatic fire, the upgraded M1918A2 could only use automatic fire, but at two rates – the original 550 rounds per minute, or 350 rounds per minute, the lower rate designed around the assumption that it would improve burst accuracy and conserve ammunition, a vital consideration for a weapon using 20-round box magazines. The gunner is in a version of the "assault fire" position, described in the field manual thus: "the automatic rifle is held with the butt under the right armpit, clasped firmly between the body and the upper portion of the arm, the sling over the left shoulder" (FM 23-5 1940: 66–68). Though being employed as an "assault fire" weapon was one of the main design considerations of the original M1918, the reality of the World War I battlefield mostly precluded such use. Nevertheless, the problem with the BAR was that despite its popularity, accuracy, and reliability (as long as it was well-maintained), it was always more an automatic rifle than a true squad light machine gun, exemplified in part by the need later in the war to add another BAR gunner to the rifle squad to make up for its limitations in providing sustained fire.

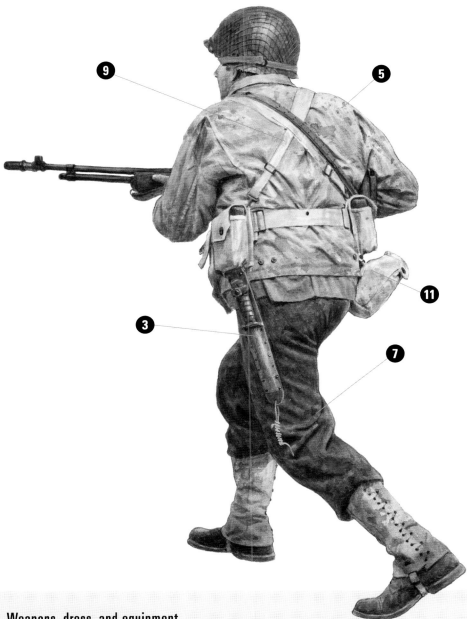

Weapons, dress, and equipment

He carries a .30-06 M1918A2 BAR (**1**) with an M1907 leather sling, this particular model being an upgraded M1918 from storage rather than a newly manufactured model, distinguishable by the screws on the magazine guides. He also carries a Mk II hand grenade (**2**) and an M3 fighting knife in an M6 sheath (**3**).

He wears an M1 helmet (**4**) covered with netting, the helmet strap looped around the back of the helmet, the helmet liner's chinstrap around the brow. His uniform consists of the ubiquitous Parsons jacket (**5**), identifiable as an earlier version by the button-flap pockets and the lack of shoulder straps, worn over a second-pattern M1942

herringbone twill jacket (**6**) and M1937 trousers (**7**; Wool, Serge, OD, Light Shade), with M1938 canvas leggings (**8**) and leather ankle-boots. His equipment consists of a set of M1936 suspenders (**9**) that help to distribute the weight of his M1937 BAR magazine belt (**10**), its six pouches capable of holding 12 20-round box magazines for the BAR (though often only eight magazines would be carried, the remaining two pouches being used for cleaning tools, spare parts, and lubricating oil). Also attached to the belt are an M1910 canteen in M1941 cover (**11**), an M1924 first-aid pouch (**12**), and his M3 knife. His weapons and equipment weigh around 45lb.

German

The two main Axis forces in Tunisia were Arnim's 5. Panzerarmee in the north and Rommel's Deutsch-Italienische Panzerarmee. Their units, principally 5. Panzerarmee's 10. Panzer-Division and Rommel's 90. leichte Afrika-Division and 21. Panzer-Division, would play a central role in the German attempt to break through II Corps' defenses in southern Tunisia.

On August 1, 1941, 21. Panzer-Division was formed by renaming 5. leichte Division; that unit had just undergone a period of strengthening and reorganization, effectively transforming it from a light-armored outfit (German *leichte Divisionen* were established in 1938, essentially being a smaller version of a proper *Panzer-Division*) into a fully capable armored division. As one of the DAK's two Panzer divisions it was in constant demand for both offensive and defensive operations, finding itself heavily engaged in all the major battles of the North African campaign including Gazala, Tobruk, Mersa Matruh, Alam el Halfa, and El Alamein. The division acted as a key element in Rommel's rearguard during the long retreat to Tunisia, its much-reduced forces usually operating as two *Kampfgruppen* (battlegroups) during the late January–early February 1943 battles around Faïd and Maknassy. On entering Tunisia it had handed over all its remaining tanks to 15. Panzer-Division on the Mareth Line, re-equipping its *Panzer-Regiment* from vehicles at Sfax in the weeks preceding Operation *Frühlingswind* (Spring Breeze), but it was still very short of *Panzergrenadiere*, only one likely understrength regiment (Panzergrenadier-Regiment 104) being available for the mid-February attack on II Corps.

Much as with 21. Panzer-Division, 90. leichte Afrika-Division's history went back to the early days of the DAK; originally formed as Divisions-Kommando zbV *Afrika* on June 26, 1941, it was an umbrella organization for existing units already serving in the North African theater, gradually increasing in size until on October 20 that same year it was renamed Afrika-Division zbV (Special Purpose Division Africa), going through several more name changes until it settled on 90. leichte Afrika-Division on July 26, 1942. To make good some of the losses suffered earlier that year it had several independent units formally attached to it in May 1942, one of them being Sonderverband 288. Formed in Potsdam on July 24, 1941, Sonderverband 288 was a special-purpose unit originally envisaged to play a part in Middle Eastern operations (it had groups of officers who spoke Greek as well as Arabic translators on its roster), but instead found itself sent to North Africa where it usually operated under the umbrella of 90. leichte Afrika-Division. Originally composed of eight companies of various types (including one of Brandenburgers – German special forces – which was quickly detached for service back in Europe), it was led by Oberst Otto Menton (a long-time close friend of Rommel) and was a strong motorized force of 1,800 personnel. Soon after it became a formal part of 90. leichte Afrika-Division it was reorganized as a *Panzergrenadier* unit, though it was not officially redesignated Panzergrenadier-Regiment *Afrika* until October 31, 1942 (and even then many still referred to it by its old name). Equipped with trucks rather than armored personnel carriers, Panzergrenadier-Regiment *Afrika* had always seen action as an infantry unit rather than as a special-operations force, fighting at Bir Hakeim,

Mersa Matruh, and El Alamein before serving as part of the *Panzerarmee's* rearguard during the retreat into Tunisia.

Unlike the perennially armor-deprived and understrength units of the DAK, at the end of 1942 10. Panzer-Division was one of the best-equipped armored units in the Wehrmacht. Withdrawn from the Soviet Union in April 1942, the division had enjoyed a period of rest and refitting in France, during which time it was brought up to its full complement of personnel and provided with the most modern weapons and vehicles available to the Heer (Army). The men of the division expected to be sent back to the Soviet Union; the first inkling they had of something different was the delivery of tropical uniforms and equipment, which started arriving in the fall of 1942. Some still thought that such uniforms might mean a campaign in the Caucasus, but soon enough all knew that North Africa was their destination. The trip across the Mediterranean was difficult and dangerous, some elements of the division never actually making it across before the final Axis collapse in May 1943. For the rest, passage was fraught with risk from naval and air attacks, both of which cost Panzer-Regiment 7 the lives of some of its men as well as a number of its tanks and other vehicles that were much-needed in North Africa and difficult to replace. Losses at sea and logistical difficulties meant that while on the eve of its departure the division had over 3,000 vehicles, fewer than 1,000 of them were successfully transported to North Africa.

ABOVE RIGHT
A highly atmospheric portrait of a German soldier in April 1941 wearing a dust scarf and a pair of Auer Neophan goggles to protect him from the harsh desert elements. Goggles and dust scarves were still useful in the more mountainous terrain and wintry conditions initially encountered in Tunisia, especially for mechanized troops who spent a lot of time in open-topped armored personnel carriers or trucks, traveling in columns that kicked up great storms of dust in dry conditions. Note also the faded *Feldmütze* cap; examples of such battered headgear came to be badges of long, active service in the desert. (Bundesarchiv Bild 101I-785-0285-14A Foto: Otto, Albrecht Heinrich)

The *Panzergrenadier* charges forward, his MG 34 machine gun held at the ready to fire from the hip if need be. Although not commonly done, firing on the move was an accepted part of the gunner's doctrine, with official instruction in field manuals as to how to go about it should the need arise (for example, the *Ausbildungsvorschrift für die Infanterie Heft 2a – Die Schützenkompanie*, "Infantry Training Regulations Book 2a – The Rifle Company," issued in 1941). When stationary, a gunner firing short bursts from the hip could expect reasonable accuracy up to 65–75yd, though such results required both strength and skill. Shooting from the hip while moving was reserved for the "last rush," where all members of the squad would be closing with the enemy, firing as they went. Unlike the figure shown here where the sling is simply looped over his right shoulder for added stability, in such a circumstance the manual called for the gunner to unclip the sling's rear buckle and then loop the now spare end of the *geteilte Trageriemen* ("divided carrying sling") over his head, tightly tucking the stock of the MG 34 under his right armpit while gripping the legs of the collapsed bipod with his left hand, though how closely such procedures were followed in field conditions is unclear.

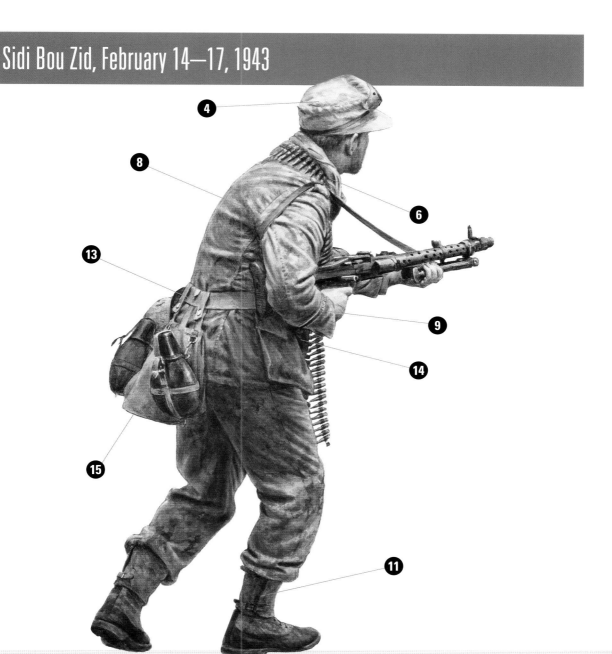

Weapons, dress, and equipment

The *Panzergrenadier* carries a 7.92mm MG 34 machine gun (**1**) suspended from a *geteilte Trageriemen* (literally "divided carrying sling") and fed by a *Gurttrommel* (belt drum; **2**), which was not technically a magazine as it just stored a standard 50-round linked belt. He also carries a 9mm Walther P 38 in a belt holster (**3**) that also stores a spare eight-round magazine for the pistol. He wears an M1941 *Tropeneinheits Feldmütze* (tropical field cap; **4**) and, as a member of a mechanized unit, he has also been issued with *Zeiss-Umbral* sun goggles (**5**) which he wears on his cap.

He wears a rough dun-colored dust scarf around his neck (**6**) that can be pulled up to protect his face from the dust of the desert. His M1935 helmet (**7**) is attached to his belt. His uniform consists of the tropical version of the M1942 *Feldbluse* (**8**) – it can be identified as a later-issued version from 1942 as the pockets have lost their pleats, but still retain their scallops, as well as the lack of *Tresse* (lace) round the collar of NCO tunics – with the Deutsches Afrikakorps *Ärmelstreifen* (cuff-title; **9**). He wears faded khaki M1940 tropical trousers (**10**) gathered into M1940 anklets (**11**) worn over a pair of second-pattern *Tropenschnürschuhe* (tropical ankle-boots; **12**). He has an M1940 tan canvas belt (**13**) with an olive-green-painted buckle on which he carries an MG 34 gunner's pouch (**14**), a bread bag with two canteens attached (**15**), and a 100-round belt of spare ammunition for his machine gun (**16**) slung over his shoulders. His weapons and equipment weigh approximately 44–50lb.

TRAINING AND TACTICS

American

The need to expand the Army meant that from March 1942 draftees were no longer centrally trained, instead being sent directly to their divisions which were thereafter made responsible for their training, following the guidelines set out in the Mobilization Training Program (Mansoor 1999: 21). This had a limited impact on the 1st and 34th Infantry divisions, however, as both were among the most battle-ready formations of the US Army and already detailed for overseas service. Shortcomings in tactical capabilities stemmed from a mixture of inadequate training, abstract doctrine, variable leadership, and general inexperience, all issues that could be remedied with attention and time. Unfortunately, one of the corollary effects of splitting up divisions and detailing their units out to widely varying commands was a concomitant interruption in ongoing training programs, the effective adoption of new weapon systems (such as the M1 Bazooka), and the development of small-unit leadership, all of which were divisional responsibilities. Even so, the performance of untried US infantry companies and battalions, sometimes poorly supported in tactically dubious deployments, was often creditable, with examples of courage and determination there for those who chose to look for them. Most importantly, the infantry would also show a willingness to learn and the flexibility to adapt to the realities of the battlefield and the behavior of their enemy.

The individual infantry units of a division were expected to operate as "combat teams," usually based around a regiment, but also employed at

A US rifleman demonstrates a form of "hasty sling" to aid in the aiming of his M1 Garand semiautomatic rifle (note also the 16in M1905 bayonet affixed to the side of his pack). In development since the mid-1920s, the Garand was adopted in 1936 and entered service the following year, meaning that the US Army was the world's only army to enter the war with a semiautomatic rifle as its standard infantry weapon. The Garand's gas-operated system allowed a soldier to maintain his sight picture more effectively than with a bolt-action rifle, to deliver follow-up shots with greater speed and accuracy, and (using the eight-round en bloc clip) reload and return to action much more quickly. The Germans had never pushed for the development of semiautomatic rifles in the same way mainly because their squad doctrine was built around the rifleman's role being to support the light machine gun, and though they fielded the Gewehr 41 (and later Gewehr 43), the designs were immature and production was low – the average German infantryman was likely to be using his five-round Kar 98k bolt-action rifle right through to the end of the war. (NARA)

An M3 medium tank with an M2 or M3 half-track serving as a radio communications vehicle in the background, pictured during the fighting near Sened, February 1943. A shortage of M4 medium tanks meant that the 1st Armored Division's 2/13th Armored was the only US battalion still equipped with the M3 during the fighting in Tunisia. Major Hans von Luck of Aufklärungs-Abteilung (mot.) 3 would see at first hand the cost that the Americans paid for their inexperience, observing the high losses a battlegroup of M4 medium tanks suffered at the hands of a much better armed and armored force of PzKpfw VI Tiger heavy tanks during an attack, admiring the courage and fighting spirit of the US tank crews even as he lamented the fact that they were having to pay such a high price for their education (Luck 2002: 142). Though many of the basic principles of combat that US forces relied upon were sound enough, their employment was hamstrung by systemic shortcomings and the inability of inexperienced commanders to overcome specific situational difficulties. There was insufficient communication and coordination between infantry, armored, and artillery units in both offensive and defensive operations, leading to misunderstandings and unnecessary losses. Control of air assets was particularly underdeveloped, allowing the Luftwaffe's local air superiority to make the running when it came to the close support of ground operations. (Eliot Elisofon/The LIFE Picture Collection/Getty Images)

the battalion level, such as at Sidi Bou Zid. A combat team consisted of an infantry regiment or battalion that was supported by artillery, armored, signals, and engineering assets, allowing it to act as a semi-independent combined-arms force that had the flexibility to operate in a range of battlefield scenarios or undertake specific tasks. The assets that were combined to make up a regimental combat team (RCT) were ideally drawn from the infantry unit's parent division (each of a division's three 105mm artillery battalions being "paired" with one of the division's three infantry regiments, for example), but the wide dispersal of the 34th and especially the 1st Infantry divisions in Tunisia made it much more difficult to form properly integrated RCTs.

The 1st Armored Division had the potential to be a powerful force, being both generally well trained and mostly equipped with the new M4A1 medium tank (one battalion was still operating with M3 medium tanks due to shortages). The practice was to divide the division up into combined-arms independent battlegroups of tanks, artillery, and armored infantry known as combat commands, with the 1st Armored Division originally having two such entities, raised to four through necessity – Combat Commands A, B, C, and D (CCC and CCD being ad hoc developments created to help manage the wide dispersal of the division's units in Tunisia). The use of combat commands showed an understanding of the utility of combined-arms formations, but there were serious deficiencies in how the elements of such commands worked together, a result of a faulty armored doctrine – one that emphasized the speed and mobility of the tank force at the expense of combined-arms formations – and inappropriate tactical training. Individual tank crews knew how to fight with their vehicles, but not how to operate at the company or battalion level against German armored tactics, nor how to mitigate their vulnerabilities and augment their advantages.

German

The US divisions were properly manned, well-equipped and well-supplied, even more so than the British and Commonwealth forces of the Eighth Army and considerably more so than the veteran units of the DAK or even the newer arrivals of 5. Panzerarmee. German *Kampfgruppe* tactics – whereby a task-specific formation was drawn together from a number of different units to create a combined-arms force of artillery, armor, and infantry – were highly developed, particularly among motorized and Panzer divisions. The men in such units were well used to reorganizing themselves, often on a daily basis, into new fighting formations that best matched the environment and enemy they were to face. This system of operation could also help to mitigate losses suffered during combat, but the reality for many mid- and late-war *Kampfgruppen* was one of necessity, where they were used to maintain at least a degree of fighting capability in formations that were desperately understrength and short on armor or artillery. Certainly some of the DAK *Kampfgruppen* that served in the Western Desert and later in Tunisia were in reality just much-reduced divisions that, through professionalism and flexibility, managed to maintain an effective fighting edge.

The Germans had developed their armored doctrine to a fine pitch in the campaigns in the Western Desert and the Soviet Union. Armored or motorized forces were usually comprised of a mix of assets, including infantry, armor, artillery, and antiaircraft elements, giving the force operational independence and flexibility. In July–August 1942 the previous designation of *Schützen* (riflemen) gave way to *Panzergrenadiere* (armored grenadiers, the latter word being an honorific bestowed on much of Germany's infantry forces in 1942) in recognition of the important role that such troops played in combined-arms operations, with motorized divisions evolving into *Panzergrenadier-Divisionen* with their own integral armored element (much like 90. leichte Afrika-Division). One of the core principles of heavily mechanized and motorized formations was the idea that they would "move separately, fight together," concentrating forces at the point of attack.

A squad of German soldiers traipse along a dusty country road in Tunisia, 1943. The gunner balances his weapon on one shoulder and carries a Patronenkasten 41 ammunition box in his left hand, extra boxes also being carried by the men in front of him, one of whom also has a Laufschützer 34 (spare-barrel carrier) slung over his shoulder. Note that they all wear the *Feldmütze* cap and carry their sand-camouflaged helmets slung on their belts, though the rest of their uniforms, boots, and equipment vary. (Bundesarchiv Bild 101I-788-0018-35A Foto: Dullin)

How an attack was conducted varied according to the nature of the objective, the terrain, and the nature of the enemy forces that would be encountered, though within such a system there were standard methodologies at play. For example, *Panzergrenadiere* would ideally be mounted in SdKfz 251 half-tracks or other armored vehicles, but the realities of battlefield losses and a lack of industrial capacity meant that in most armored or motorized divisions only one battalion would be so equipped, the rest of the men transported in trucks. Aside from having limited off-road capabilities, truck-bound infantry had to adapt their tactics to their poorer level of protection and maneuverability, ideally dismounting under cover (or at least concealment) out of range of the enemy. Half-track-equipped *Panzergrenadiere* could remain closer to the armored element of their *Kampfgruppen*, but they were not expected to fight side by side with the tanks, and they too had to take care during deployment of their *Panzergrenadiere*. Once the troops had dismounted, each vehicle (usually equipped with at least a light machine gun) could provide mobile fire support to its infantry component.

Armored units were well-experienced in tank combat, using a variety of techniques including *Panzerwarte* ("tank ambush") to inflict maximum damage on an opponent. Ambushes were set up with one force of tanks (often in retreat) acting as the lure, drawing an enemy force onward into a predetermined killing ground that was lined with Panzers usually *halbverdeckte* ("semi-concealed") behind terrain features, working in conjunction with screens of well-camouflaged antitank guns. If possible, air strikes by the Luftwaffe would be employed to attack the main enemy force or to harry its supporting elements.

A German crew (note the broad variation in cap shades) prepare their 7.5cm leichtes Infanteriegeschütz 18 infantry-support gun for action. In *Panzergrenadier* formations the 880lb leIG 18 was towed by an SdKfz 251/4 prime mover and operated by a crew of six; it could fire 8–12 rounds per minute, including shells with limited armor-piercing capability out to a maximum range of 300m (328yd), though it usually fired 6kg (13.23lb) high-explosive shells out to a maximum range of 3,550m (3,882yd). (AirSeaLand Photos)

LOGISTICS AND MORALE

American

Though the US war effort would come to be synonymous with limitless supplies, the situation was not quite so rosy in North Africa. The factories and arsenals of the United States were developing at an ever-increasing rate, but the demands for their goods and weapons were enormous, encompassing the rapid and massive expansion of the US armed forces as well as the need to support allies, especially Britain and the Soviet Union. This led to real shortages, resulting in one tank battalion of the 1st Armored Division being equipped with older M3 medium tanks rather than the newer M4 because a number of the latter were needed by the Eighth Army. Such realities aside, II Corps was generally very well equipped and armed, though a logistical learning curve meant that the supplies did not always get to where they needed to be in a timely fashion. For the Germans the American situation was one to be envied; Major Hans von Luck was among those who marveled at the speed with which every sort of American supply deficiency seemed to be remedied, the excellent weapons (including first-class tanks and antitank guns) with which their units were equipped, and also the average soldier's daily rations of chewing gum, chocolate, cigarettes, and butter that they found on some of the prisoners from the 34th Infantry Division they had taken at Kasserine – rare luxuries for a German soldier (Luck 2002: 142).

There was no escaping the fact that life on the Tunisian front was often harsh. Winter was the rainy season, and though temperatures rarely dropped as low as 32°F, the environment could be damp and was often suffused with a miserable bone-biting chill that wore men down. The war correspondent Ernie Pyle noted the importance of simple comforts in such places, offering a soldier $50 for a small old-fashioned kerosene stove that would probably only cost $3 back in the States. The soldier refused, and Pyle understood why – money's no use when you're cold at night (Nichols 1986: 84). Food supply was another issue; though troops did not usually go hungry, they often had to rely on cold C-rations (tinned meals notorious for their bland taste that became monotonous all too quickly) for days, sometimes weeks at a time, with proper hot meals few and far between.

Despite the presence of a smattering of regular soldiers and wartime volunteers, the average infantryman serving in the 1st or 34th Infantry divisions was likely to be a draftee, still getting used to the rigors of Army life and unfamiliar with the practicalities of campaigning, let alone the horrible realities of warfare. Such inexperience went some way to explain the panic that ensued after the early defeats inflicted by the Germans, particularly at Sidi Bou Zid and Kasserine, though in both those cases the tactical reality on the ground would have challenged the nerve of more experienced men. Despite such defeats (in large part due to operational failings on the part of divisional and corps commanders and their staffs), many of the officers at regimental level and below were competent men who earned the trust of the soldiers in their care. Being mostly conscripted into service the men themselves were not necessarily motivated by patriotism or professional pride, though the latter would develop along with the reputations of successful units; rather, small-

unit cohesion – the trust and care that men in companies and platoons placed in one another – would prove to be one of the most important reasons why they fought effectively, as well as the sense of being an integral part of a larger whole, something badly damaged by the wanton distribution of individual units with no regard to the identity of their parent regiments or divisions.

German

The Panzer divisions of the Heer, having been at war for over three years, had amassed a considerable degree of experience that the newly arrived Americans could not hope to match. Such experience – operational and tactical – permeated every level of the DAK and the units of 5. Panzerarmee, most of their officers and men having learned their lessons again and again in the field. The high level of success enjoyed by German operations was proof of their skill, but it also masked some serious failings. The Heer's logistical system was inadequate for anything beyond a lightning campaign, demonstrated most glaringly during the invasion of the Soviet Union in 1941, and never properly addressed afterward. The DAK as well as 5. Panzerarmee knew how to adapt to shortages, making the most of captured vehicles and matériel, but there came a point where a lack of tanks, ammunition, or fuel could not be mitigated with creative thinking. Logistical difficulties would have real operational consequences for Rommel and Arnim, playing a direct role in strategic decisions (Rommel's plan to advance on Tébessa in Algeria, for example, being driven in no small part by the prospect of capturing the vast Allied supply dumps that were located there).

The German troops confronting the Americans in Tunisia were tried-and-tested men. The DAK divisions had been in combat for the best part of two

US Army sergeants George McGray (at left) and Bernard Haber checking their map during a hard drive through poor conditions, February 1, 1943. The war correspondent Ernie Pyle lived alongside the GIs on the front lines and reported on the everyday toll taken by simply sustaining some semblance of daily life, never mind from the actual fighting. The harsh environment, little sleep, cold food, and constant hard work wore soldiers down, Pyle observing that such an existence quickly altered one's perspective on what mattered. His reportage gave the war a measurable human presence for his readers in the United States, a reassuring counterweight to the more abstract talk of battles and commanders that usually prevailed. (Eliot Elisofon/The LIFE Picture Collection/Getty Images)

years, fighting determined British and Commonwealth forces back and forth across most of North Africa. This had led to the development of a strong *esprit de corps*, most soldiers taking great pride in their service in what had become a renowned fighting force. They wore their "Afrikakorps" cuff-titles and painted the DAK's swastika-and-palm-tree symbol on their vehicles (often leaving the symbol uncovered when they painted their helmets with camouflage), very much seeing themselves as having earned their elite status. They also had great confidence and pride in their commander Erwin Rommel, at 50 years of age the youngest *Generalfeldmarschall* in the Wehrmacht at the time of his promotion on June 21, 1942, and a man of proven ability in battle after battle. Rommel was also keenly aware of the importance of being seen by his men, especially on the front lines, where his presence boosted morale and aided in the sense that all were fighting for the same things, and sharing the same risks while doing so.

Though 10. Panzer-Division (along with the rest of 5. Panzerarmee) was new to North Africa, only arriving in December 1942, it was a unit with considerable experience in a number of European campaigns, having taken part in the invasions of Poland, France, and the Soviet Union, where it participated in some extremely harsh fighting on the Eastern Front during Operation *Barbarossa* and the subsequent grim winter of 1941–42. The unit's men had a strong sense of *Kampfgeist* ("battle spirit"), derived from the hardships they had endured and the successes they had achieved; such spirit would be demonstrated in their professional and uncompromising engagements with US forces.

COMMAND

American

The rapid expansion of the US Army from 1940 (which had a total of only 14,000 officers by the end of that year) had taken a toll on its already rather sclerotic leadership. Many of the junior officers and newly minted NCOs lacked confidence, while others, particularly in National Guard units, were either too old or were unqualified for their roles (Mansoor 1999: 19). There was no quick remedy for this problem, and its effects were felt throughout the Army during its early engagements in North Africa, Sicily, and Italy. In addition, the training in leadership that such officers received had grown out of doctrine that had been developed mostly throughout the 1930s (found in the US War Department's Field Manual 100-5), though many of its strictures were not fully realized. Too often lessons were only understood in the abstract, with many of the instructors not having much more experience than the men they were training, this being an inevitable situation in a small peacetime army that was expanding enormously and with great rapidity. Despite these shortcomings, the battles in Tunisia during February and March 1943 would often show company and battalion commanders performing well in very trying circumstances, though their effectiveness was often limited by the haphazard coordination of forces and poor direction from divisional and corps commands.

The situation for their more senior counterparts also suffered from growing pains, as such men rarely had the experience to run, maneuver, and fight large formations with any degree of success, something exposed during the Louisiana and Carolina maneuvers in 1941 in which the majority of divisional and corps commanders proved to be unfit for a host of different reasons. In 1941 there were no serving officers with experience of running a division from World War I (Atkinson 2002: 10). The prewar regular Army had been a relatively small affair, with little room for promotion to senior rank or the commensurate chance to command large bodies of troops, or even to serve within such a body and see how major formations were managed and fought. Many of those regular Army officers who had spent long years as majors (average age: 48) or lieutenant colonels suddenly found themselves with the chance to run division-sized formations, and as the Army had no better candidates, run them they did. As the war progressed the more obviously unfit candidates would be weeded out and replaced by a newer generation of much more capable men, but such decisions usually had to be made in the wake of actual performance, and thus could take some time.

The mix of inexperienced commanders leading formations of untried men led many officers to approach their duties with cautiousness; an understandable approach but one that would have repercussions. There was a general lack of trust in subordinates that started at the top and filtered its way down, exemplified by Fredendall's micromanagement and the reluctance of the officers at divisional and regimental levels below him to exercise their own initiative. Trapped on Djebel Garet Hadid (djebel = hill) on the first day of fighting in the battle of Sidi Bou Zid in February 1943, Colonel Thomas D. Drake had radioed for permission to abandon his position that

was rapidly being enveloped; his request went to Brigadier General Raymond E. McQuillin, the commander of CCA at Sidi Bou Zid a few miles from Garet Hadid, who passed Drake's message on to Major General Orlando Ward, the commander of the 1st Armored Division at Sbeïtla, 20 miles away from the battle, who in turn sent it on to Fredendall at II Corps headquarters over 80 miles behind the front. Fredendall refused Drake permission to withdraw despite the fact that he could have no clear sense of the situation "on the ground." Although much blame can be laid at the door of Fredendall's personality, the hesitancy of the officers under his command to act on their own initiative was in part likely derived from a military culture that encouraged reliance on structures and hierarchy, dissuading officers from engaging with the risks and consequences of independent action.

German

There was considerable friction between Rommel and Arnim, Kesselring having to act as referee on more than one occasion. Rommel undervalued Arnim's caution, especially in regard to the importance of logistics and a sustainable supply line in the transformation of an initial victory into an effective and deep exploitation. The obvious rivalry between Kesselring's two commanders led him to simplify the chain of command, putting Rommel in charge of all Axis troops in Tunisia, though this evolution (encouraged by Rommel himself) didn't come to pass until early March 1943, its efficacy being somewhat undermined by Rommel's departure from the theater on March 9 due to "exhaustion."

Battlefield leadership of divisions and *Kampfgruppen* was generally effective, their commanders having a great deal of experience in those roles, though their successes were often limited by the logistical realities of their operations. German combat leadership was well-developed and usually very effective, being the result of a doctrine that had been nurtured before the outbreak of war in field manuals like *Truppenführung* (1933, 1934).

That doctrine put a premium on boldness and daring preceded by good judgment, encouraging independent thought and resourcefulness at all levels of leadership, from division to platoon. Mission objectives were determined by one's superiors, but the methods by which they were achieved (usually known as *Auftragstaktik*, mission-oriented tactics) were the responsibility of the officer or NCO detailed to undertake the tasks. Orders were expected to be obeyed though not adhered to slavishly or in spite of reality, as it was recognized that quirks of circumstance or the natural dynamism that was one of the defining characteristics of a battlefield could make impromptu re-evaluations necessary. The old Prussian ideal of aggressiveness in the face of the enemy, taking the fight to him at every opportunity with the intention of destroying his ability to resist, underpinned German warfighting doctrine and ensured that infantry and armored tactics were combative without being hidebound.

The nurturing of effective leadership was well-managed in German NCO and officer schools, though the years of development that went into the selection and teaching of such men was starting to become something of a luxury by early 1943. The premium that such an education put on leading by example, often from the front, resulted in high numbers of casualties that were increasingly difficult to replace. Junior officers and NCOs were trained as a matter of course to be able to do the job of their immediate superior should the need arise, and many formations were led, often for prolonged periods, by men of relatively low rank who had demonstrated the capability to do so.

Generalfeldmarschall Erwin Rommel conferring with his staff at the front in early March 1943, just prior to his evacuation from the Tunisian theater due to "exhaustion." A gifted tactician and highly popular commander with his men (and a number of his enemies), Rommel suffered from the confusing levels of command exercised over Axis forces in North Africa, and was often frustrated with the different priorities and cautious approach of his fellow officer Generaloberst Hans-Jürgen von Arnim, commander of 5. Panzerarmee. (LAPI/Roger Viollet/Getty Images)

COMMUNICATIONS

American

Generally, the most stable and secure method of communication was through a field telephone system, though the wires such a system relied upon were always its weakest link, being vulnerable to artillery fire and other mishaps. The standard model was the EE-8 field telephone, which was battery-powered and had a range of either 5 or 14 miles depending on the cable used, and which would be connected to a switchboard system at battalion, regimental, or divisional level. Radios were more flexible but suffered from a range of problems including poor batteries, bad weather, jamming, interference, and interception (Sayen 2006: 56). The experiences of the various units of the 168th Infantry Regiment at Sidi Bou Zid give a good sense of how fractious radio communications could be, the battalions there enduring regular problems in getting through to other units or higher commands, one example (Colonel Thomas Drake on Djebel Garet Hadid) being where the radio would usually work during the day but the signal would fade away to nothing as darkness fell. Poor communications security significantly exacerbated the problems caused by enemy eavesdropping, with much important information of both an operational and tactical nature being overheard by the Germans during the battles around Kasserine thanks to dismal message discipline in US forces (particularly the 1st Armored Division), with some transmissions about mission-critical matters being made "in the clear," i.e. entirely unencoded.

Smoke rises from a knocked-out half-track in the background while American infantrymen dig foxholes during the Allied raid on Sened. The M3 was a highly versatile vehicle, operating as an infantry carrier, command vehicle, self-propelled artillery mount, and tank destroyer, among other roles. The M1897A4 75mm guns mounted on the M3 GMCs of units like the 701st Tank Destroyer Battalion packed a decent enough punch, but the thin armor of the vehicles (.25in face-hardened steel plate, increased to .5in for the windshield protective plate) was totally inadequate against Panzers or antitank guns. The doctrine determining the effective use of such vehicles also left much to be desired. (Eliot Elisofon/The LIFE Picture Collection/Getty Images)

The SCR (Set, Complete, Radio) systems included the SCR-536 (the "handie-talkie" AM set with a 1.5-mile range); the SCR-508 and SCR-608 (both vehicle-mounted FM sets with a 10-mile range); and the SCR-284 (maximum continuous-wave range of 25 miles) for the divisional headquarters. At the start of the war all sets used AM frequencies, but during the North African campaign new sets that could use the considerably better FM frequencies began to make an appearance, though it would not be until 1944 that their use became widespread. At company level a communications net was made up of SCR-536s (one for the commander, one each for his platoon commanders, and one at the company command post), as well as telephones connected to observation posts and the battalion HQ. Battalions and regiments had their own dedicated communications platoons (a regiment, for example, had three communications platoons, one for each battalion, each platoon having a message center, a wire section, and a radio section) that relied on (semi) portable telephone switchboards capable of handling 6 (BD-71), 12 (BD-72) or 40 (BD-14) lines as well as a range of both man-portable, ground, and vehicle-mounted radios, though messaging between companies and battalions often still relied on messengers, picked men who were chosen for their sense, intelligence, and skill.

German

German man-portable radios were designated as *Tornister Funkgerät* ("backpack radio equipment"), usually abbreviated to "TornFu" followed by a lower-case letter and a number to designate the type or modification of radio in use. *Feld Funkgerät* ("field radio equipment"; FeldFu) referred to portable and stationary radios, while radio sets mounted in vehicles were simply called *Funkgerät* ("radio equipment"; Fu). The TornFuG ("*Tornister Funkgerät* Gustav") was an excellent radio used by *Panzergrenadiere* to maintain contact with their half-tracks. Its frequency coverage was 2.5–3.5MHz with a 1.5-watt power output. It used a whip antenna, could be carried by one man (40lb), and operated on the move. The standard radio at regimental level and below was the 39lb TornFu Dora or Dora2, which could also be operated on the move (one man carrying the transceiver, another the battery pack) and had a voice range of 4 miles and a Morse range of 9.5 miles. The main German field telephone was the Feldfernsprecher 33, which weighed 12lb and connected to the ten-line battalion switchboard (kleiner Klappenschrank zu 10 Leitungen) or the 20-line regimental switchboard (Feldklappenschrank zu 20 Leitungen).

A *Grenadier-Regiment's* signals unit would have two 20-line switchboards each with four telephones, four more telephones in two light telephone units, and four TornFu d2 transceiver radios, while an infantry battalion would usually have four telephones and four TornFu d2 radios. Armored and *Panzergrenadier* units had a much greater number of radios at their disposal in recognition of the vital role that communications played in how they were expected to maneuver and fight, with all tanks and a large number of armored personnel carriers and reconnaissance vehicles equipped with sets of one sort or another, including dedicated command-and-communications vehicles. *Panzergrenadier* units that were fully mechanized

would be equipped with an SdKfz 251/3 mittlerer Kommandopanzerwagen/Funkpanzerwagen ("command/communications vehicle"), while the *Panzer-Nachrichten-Abteilung* would use vehicles such as the SdKfz 251/19 *Fernsprechbetriebspanzerwagen* ("telephone exchange vehicle"). Other elements including reconnaissance and motorized forces would have used vehicles like the six-wheel SdKfz 232 (easily recognizable due to its highly distinctive *Rahmenantenne* "loop" aerial that was nicknamed the "bedspread" and which stretched over the vehicle's hull) which carried a FuGer 11 SE 100 medium-range and a FuSprGer A short-range radio. Also common was the eight-wheel SdKfz 232 that used a more discreet *Sternantenne* ("star aerial") for its medium-range radios, or the SdKfz 263 (8-rad) which was a dedicated communications vehicle that retained the *Rahmenantenne* aerial as well as a 9-meter *Kurbelmast* telescoping aerial, carrying one Sätz Funkgerät für (m) Pz Funktrupp b radio.

All tanks within German armored units were equipped with radios, each *Panzer-Kompanie* having a dedicated command-and-communications tank, though the *Panzertruppen* also used more rudimentary communications when the situation demanded it, including signal flags, hand signals, flares, flashlights, and hand smoke signals. Flags were unpopular, being seen as too conspicuous, with hand signals being used when other units were in very close proximity. Smoke signals (and flares at night) were used to signal accompanying infantry and artillery units, and were color-coded to convey simple meanings such as "We are attacking," "We are cut off," or "Enemy tanks ahead."

Sidi Bou Zid

February 14–17, 1943

BACKGROUND TO BATTLE

The situation facing Generalfeldmarschall Rommel as January 1943 drew to a close was serious but stable. He had outrun the British Eighth Army in the south, and Lieutenant-General Anderson's First Army, with too much ground to defend and bogged down in Tunisia's short rainy season, had stalled on the edge of the Eastern Dorsal. Without control of the passes through the mountain range it would be much more difficult for Rommel and Generaloberst von Arnim to defend against an Allied incursion onto the coastal plain, and next to impossible for them to prosecute a successful campaign of their own. To that end strong elements of 21. and 10. Panzer-Divisionen launched attacks to seize positions around Pichon and the Faïd Pass on January 30, quickly overwhelming the 1,000 poorly equipped French troops who held the pass despite a valiant defense.

Orders quickly came down from Anderson that the German incursion must be thrown back. Initial US hopes were high; a raid on the village of Sened on January 24 had proved to be a success, with 96 prisoners taken for no loss of American life, boosting their sense of their own capabilities as well as the weakness of the enemy. A task force led by Colonel Alexander N. Stark, comprising the 1st Infantry Division's 26th Regimental Combat Team (less the 2/26th and 3/26th Infantry), supported by the 3/1st Armored and the 701st Tank Destroyer Battalion from CCA, was quickly pulled together and attempted to relieve the Faïd Pass on January 31, while a similar force led by Colonel William B. Kern moved against the Rebaou Pass at the same time. The results were quite different from those of the raid on Sened: the Americans were too late to save the French, and their forces proved too small to dislodge the Germans who had established strong defenses in the interim. The Americans assaulted again the following day, but to no avail. The Faïd Pass was firmly in German hands. The overall performance of all the US units involved left much to be desired, the whole enterprise having suffered from indifferent planning, incoherent chains of command, and poor communications. The attacking forces themselves displayed poor coordination between infantry and armor (some of which got bogged down), as well as an inability to concentrate their forces or press home their attacks – deficiencies that the Germans noticed. The reversal at the Faïd Pass stalled future Allied initiatives, with II Corps moving to a defensive posture, but had exactly the opposite effect on the Germans, who now saw vulnerabilities that were ripe for exploitation.

In the wake of the capture of the Faïd Pass and the poor showing of the elements of II Corps that had tried to thwart the German attacks, Rommel proposed a major operation to break through the American lines with the objective of seizing the main Allied supply center just over the Algerian border at Tébessa. This would not only cause II Corps major logistical problems, it would also leave the Germans in a good position to swing north and threaten Bône on the northern coast. Arnim had a more conservative view, feeling that there simply were not the troops, ammunition, and fuel to accomplish such a major strategic victory. Instead, he suggested limiting the objective to pushing American forces back into the Western Dorsal; that would remove the looming threat they posed to the rear of Rommel's Afrikakorps, as well as spoiling any attempt they might have made to launch an attack on Tunis. Generalfeldmarschall Kesselring, acting as the arbiter between his two commanders as well as being responsible for persuading the Comando Supremo to approve any plan of action, favored Arnim's safer approach, but encouraged Rommel to believe that should the situation on the ground develop with unexpected success, more ambitious goals could still be sought. The plan called for two thrusts: Rommel would move against Gafsa in Operation *Morgenluft* (Morning Air), while Arnim would break through the passes at Faïd and Maïzila and capture Sidi Bou Zid in Operation *Frühlingswind* (Spring Breeze). After some delay due to the complexities of getting command approval for such an operation, the morning of February 14 was chosen as the day of the attack.

Arnim's force for *Frühlingswind* consisted of 10. Panzer-Division and the DAK veterans of 21. Panzer-Division, and was commanded by Generalleutnant Heinz Ziegler. Tasked with penetrating through the Faïd

A 105mm T19 Howitzer Motor Carriage (HMC) with accompanying jeep; part of the T19's ammunition limber can be seen to the left, where an artillerist is transferring a 105mm shell to the gun's crew (the T19 only carried eight rounds with the gun). Built on the chassis of an M3 half-track, the T19 was armed with a 105mm M2A1 howitzer and was protected by a .25in armored gun plate, good enough for deflecting small-arms fire and light shrapnel but little else. The self-propelled guns were something of a stopgap design and were usually found assigned to the headquarters elements of armored divisions as well as their armored field-artillery battalions, or the cannon companies of infantry divisions. Used throughout the Tunisian campaign, most T19s had been replaced in armored units with the 105mm M7 HMC "Priest" by the time of the invasion of Sicily in July 1943, though their presence continued a little longer among the infantry. (Eliot Elisofon/The LIFE Picture Collection/Getty Images)

Pass along Highway 13 and enveloping Sidi Bou Zid from the north, 10. Panzer-Division was divided into three groups for the operation with around 119 tanks between them: two *Angriffsgruppen* (attacking groups), one led by Panzergrenadier-Regiment 86's commander, Oberst Hans Reimann, the other by Oberst Rudolf Gerhardt, and a reserve *Kampfgruppe* commanded by Panzergrenadier-Regiment 69's commander, Oberst Rudolf Lang. Kampfgruppe *Reimann* comprised Panzergrenadier-Regiment 86 (less I./PzGrenRgt 86), plus one company from schwere Panzer-Abteilung 501 (six PzKpfw VI Tiger heavy tanks and nine PzKpfw III medium tanks), one *Zug* from 3./PzPiBtl 49 (to clear mines), 1./PzJgAbt 90 (less one platoon), an assault-gun battery from Panzer-Artillerie-Regiment 90, and one antiaircraft platoon of 12./PzArtRgt 90. Kampfgruppe *Gerhardt* comprised Panzer-Regiment 7 (less II./PzRgt 7), II./PzGrenRgt 69, 3./PzPiBtl 49 (less one platoon), 3./PzJgAbt 90 (less one platoon), one platoon from 1./PzJgAbt 90, and one battery of 10.5cm leFH 18 light howitzers from Panzer-Artillerie-Regiment 90. Kampfgruppe *Lang* comprised Kradschützen-Bataillon 10, Panzer-Pionier-Bataillon 49 (less one company), one platoon from 3./PzJgAbt 90, and two antiaircraft combat teams from Panzer-Artillerie-Regiment 90 (Schick 2013: 462).

Tasked with breaching the Maïzila Pass and enveloping Sidi Bou Zid from the south, 21. Panzer-Division fielded two striking forces. Kampfgruppe *Schütte* included one battalion from Panzer-Regiment 5, the *Stabs-Kompanie* of Panzergrenadier-Regiment 104, Panzerjäger-Abteilung 39/609, I./PzArtRgt 155 (less 1. and 3. Batterien), and one 8.8cm-equipped *Flakkampftruppe* (antiaircraft combat section), while Kampfgruppe *Stenkhoff* deployed one battalion from Panzer-Regiment 5, the rest of Panzergrenadier-Regiment 104, the *Stabs-Kompanie* of III./PzArtRgt 155, and two 8.8cm-equipped *Flakkampftruppe*). Kampfgruppe *Schütte* would advance up Highway 83 toward Sidi Bou Zid, while Kampfgruppe *Stenkhoff* was to drive west until it hit the Gafsa–Hadjeb el Aïoun road, whereupon it would hook around and head back toward Sidi Bou Zid along Highway 125, allowing the *Kampfgruppen* to attack the town from both the southeast and southwest, complementing 10. Panzer-Division's northern envelopment. Between them, 21. Panzer-Division's two groups had around 91 tanks. The remaining German artillery from both divisions was set up in the hills to the east of the Faïd and Maïzila passes in support of the attack.

MAP KEY

1   0400hrs, February 14: Four German *Kampfgruppen* begin their assault through the Faïd and Maïzila passes.

2   0600hrs, February 14: Kampfgruppe *Gerhardt* encounters and destroys the small screening force at the base of Djebel Lessouda.

3   0830hrs, February 14: Djebel Lessouda is encircled by Kampfgruppe *Reimann* and Kampfgruppe *Gerhardt*.

4   c.0900hrs, February 14: Seeing the advance of Kampfgruppe *Schütte* up Highway 83, Colonel Thomas D. Drake on Djebel Ksaira splits his command, taking a force to secure Djebel Garet Hadid. His forces come under attack, but hold out. Soon his positions are surrounded.

5   0930hrs, February 14: Lieutenant Colonel Louis V. Hightower's armored reaction force engages Kampfgruppe *Reimann* and Kampfgruppe *Gerhardt* in a delaying action. By midday Hightower's command is effectively destroyed. Brigadier General Raymond E. McQuillin's CCA retreats to

the northwest. The first German elements enter Sidi Bou Zid around 1300hrs and by 1705hrs the spearheads of 21. Panzer-Division and 10. Panzer-Division connect to the west of the town on Highway 125.

6   1540hrs, February 15: Colonel Robert I. Stack leads an armored battlegroup from the 1st Armored Division in an attempt to break through the German forces at Sidi Bou Zid and relieve the US infantry on Djebel Lessouda, Djebel Ksaira, and Djebel Garet Hadid. Stack's force is mostly destroyed, the remnants withdrawing at 1740hrs.

7   2200hrs, February 15: Major Robert R. Moore leads his men off Djebel Lessouda in a bold attempt to get back to American lines; ultimately 432 survivors make it back.

8   2200hrs, February 16: Colonel Drake's command begins its attempt to break out from Djebel Garet Hadid and Djebel Ksaira; having successfully evaded the enemy throughout the night, at daybreak on February 17 his force is caught in the open by an armored column, which overwhelms the Americans.

Battlefield environment

Once an enemy force was through the Faïd and Maïzila passes the ground on the approach to Sidi Bou Zid was ideal for mechanized formations, being mostly flat and free of the stone-dotted terrain that was so common in the Eastern Dorsal. The roads were narrow, little more than strips of packed earth; one road, Highway 13, led through the Faïd Pass, past the southern edge of Djebel Lessouda and on to what would become known as "Kern's Crossroads" and eventually to Sbeïtla. Another road, Highway 83, ran north from the Maïzila Pass, past the western edge of Djebel Ksaira and on to Sidi Bou Zid. Djebel Lessouda, Djebel Ksaira, Djebel Garet Hadid, and Djebel Hamra were, as far as the

Americans were concerned, the key features of the landscape, hardscrabble low hills that rose out of a confusion of gullies and loose rock; the stony ground made them difficult to fortify, entrenchments mostly giving way to built-up rock walls using the plentiful scree that lay all about. A series of three wadis scarred the ground near Sidi Salem, a major obstacle to armored movement. There was little other cover, either on the hills or the plain, with vegetation limited to coarse cactus, clump grass, and patches of thorn-infested camel brush, but there were stretches of dead ground and enough variation in the lie of the land to offer the sort of opportunities that an experienced attacker could exploit.

An M4A1 medium tank from G/1st Armored tows a disabled M3 half-track off the battlefield near the village of Sidi Bou Zid, February 1943. Djebel Lessouda, where Lieutenant Colonel John K. Waters' command post was situated together with Major Robert R. Moore's 2/168th Infantry, can be seen quite clearly in the background, standing out from the flat ground lying to the west of the Faïd and Maïzila passes. (NARA)

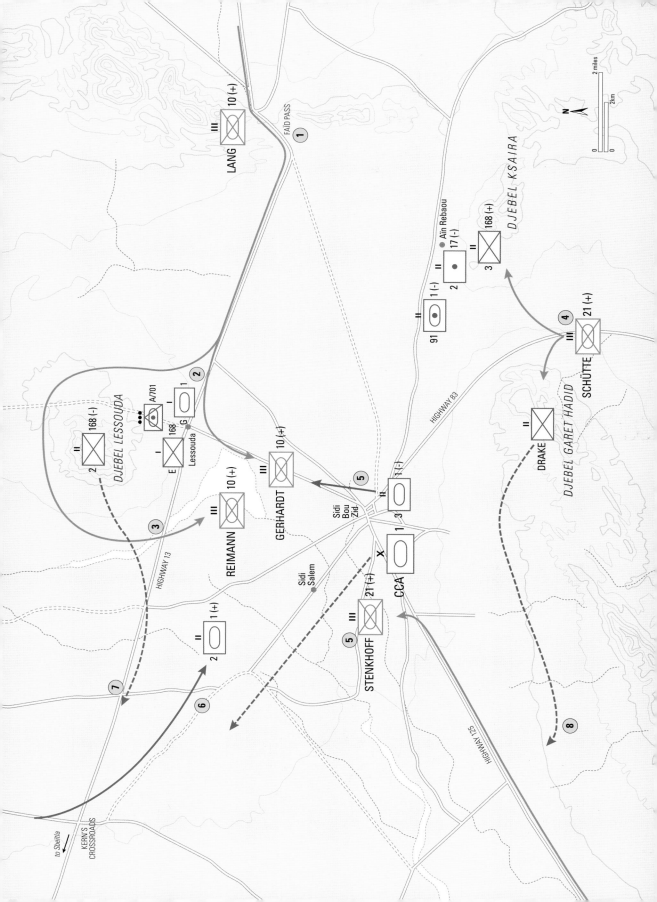

FAID PASS

LANG
III
10 (+)

(1)

DJEBEL KSAIRA

Aïn Rebaou

II 168 (+)
3

II 17 (-)
2

II 1 (-)
91

(4)

SCHÜTTE
III 21 (+)

HIGHWAY 83

2 miles

2km

N

DJEBEL LESSOUDA

(2)

A/701

I 1
G

I 168
E Lessouda

II 168 (-)
2

(3)

REIMANN
III 10 (+)

GERHARDT
III 10 (+)

(5)

II 1 (-)
3

Sidi Bou Zid.

DRAKE
II

DJEBEL GARET HADID

HIGHWAY 13

Sidi Salem

X

CCA
1 3

(6)

(8)

II 1 (+)
2

STENKHOFF
III 21 (+)

(5)

(7)

HIGHWAY 125

KERN'S CROSSROADS

to Sbeïtla

INTO COMBAT

Originally from Major General Ryder's 34th Infantry Division, the 168th Regimental Combat Team (less the 1/168th Infantry and the regiment's antitank and engineer companies) had moved recently from its role guarding lines of communication near Constantine to take up new positions in the area around Gafsa–Sbeïtla on January 29, where it was placed under the command of Major General Ward's 1st Armored Division. On February 8 it was detailed to relieve the 1st Infantry Division's 26th Regimental Combat Team at Sidi Bou Zid. In reality never much more than a battalion combat team, the 1/26th Infantry had lost 120 men during the battles at the Faïd Pass and was in need of rest and refitting, pulling back to Sbeïtla. Such unit shuffling was par for the course in Major General Fredendall's II Corps, which was strung out along the length of the Western Dorsal, defending against any Axis incursion. US units were distributed piecemeal all down the line, most divisions seeing their regiments and battalions parceled out on an ad hoc basis to widely disparate locations, often detailed to cover areas far larger than they could handle. The deployment defending the Faïd Pass was typical, with Fredendall himself personally responsible for detailing the exact positions that Major General Ward's infantry and armor were to assume, much to Ward's despair.

Fredendall's plan of defense assumed that infantry, positioned on hills near the pass, would slow down an attacking force, allowing an armored counterattack to be launched from Sidi Bou Zid. Two large hills flanked the road from the pass to Sidi Bou Zid, Djebel Lessouda to the north and Djebel Ksaira to the south, and it was here that the US infantry were to be sited, one battalion with supporting elements on each hill. The fact that they were over 10 miles away from each other – obvious to anyone on the ground, but not perhaps to Fredendall making his decisions based only on maps – ensured that they would be unable to provide mutual support in the event of an Axis attack. In addition, the isolated nature of the hills and the relatively modest units occupying them meant that the defenders were too weak to dominate the valley and thus force an attacker into confronting the threat that they posed; a clever enemy would simply bypass them.

Djebel Lessouda was occupied by Lieutenant Colonel John K. Waters' command element (consisting of Waters himself, two drivers for a jeep and M3 command half-track, and a staff officer) that was established in a sheltered wadi-ravine on the south side of the hill, while Major Robert R. Moore, an officer still getting used to his new command, led the 2/168th Infantry (646 men strong, less E/168th Infantry, with two platoons of H/168th Infantry attached) on the heights. Around 10 miles to the south, Djebel Ksaira was occupied by Colonel Thomas D. Drake, whose command included the 3/168th Infantry and an engineer platoon from C/109th Engineer Combat Battalion, both from the 34th Infantry Division, plus a tank-destroyer unit and the 39th Infantry Regiment's Cannon Company, both from 9th Infantry Division. Eight T19 HMCs of the 91st Armored Field Artillery Battalion (less Battery B) and 12 towed 155mm guns of the 2/17th FAR were placed at the base of Djebel Ksaira astride the Sidi Bou Zid–Aïn Rebaou road. On the night of February 12/13, a draft of infantry replacements arrived, but it soon

turned out that they were a mix of medics, gunners, and tank-destroyer crews; some did not even have rifles, all were lacking bayonets and entrenching tools, and many of them had never even fired a weapon, let alone been properly trained in infantry tactics. Nevertheless, they were parceled out between the battalion companies just as six truckloads of bazookas arrived; in hindsight a most auspicious weapon, except that nobody knew how to use them – no training had been given to any of the units in the 168th Regimental Combat Team despite several months'-worth of repeated requests.

The inexperience of the 168th Infantry Regiment's men and officers was compounded by a lack of equipment; this was demonstrated by the simple preparations of their positions, with Djebel Lessouda and Djebel Ksaira being only lightly fortified by wire entanglements, with a small single minefield laid to the east of the latter. A modest armored screening force made up of the seven tanks of G/1st Armored was positioned on the plain at the foot of Djebel Lessouda, supported by an infantry platoon from E/168th Infantry and two platoons from H/168th Infantry, as well as a platoon of 75mm M3 GMC (Gun Motor Carriage) tank destroyers from A/701st TDB and a few pieces of 105mm armored artillery; the small unit was to give early warning of an attack and was connected by tank radio to Waters in his command post on the southern slope of Djebel Lessouda. Officers from 10. Panzer-Division observed the screening force from a forward command post they had established in the mountains on February 13: they counted 14 tanks out in the open, uncamouflaged and lined up in formation (Schick 2013: 463).

Support was provided by Lieutenant Colonel Louis V. Hightower's armored reaction force stationed by Sidi Bou Zid, which included M4 medium tanks from H/1st Armored and I/1st Armored, as well as approximately 12 M3 GMCs from the 701st Tank Destroyer Battalion. Brigadier General McQuillin, commanding CCA, 1st Armored Division, had his headquarters in Sidi Bou Zid, while Ward's 1st Armored Division headquarters was near Sbeïtla, around 24 miles farther to the west up Highway 13. A further reserve was made up

An M4A1 medium tank powers along a dusty Tunisian plain. The M4 (and M4A1, the difference being the method of turret manufacture – the M4's was welded and the M4A1's was cast) was an excellent all-round tank, and one well capable of holding its own against PzKpfw III and IV medium tanks, its good frontal protection and 75mm gun making it a potentially lethal threat to the German Panzers. Nevertheless the M4s suffered appalling losses at Sidi Bou Zid, though it was through no fault of the vehicles; the crews were well-trained in how to operate their tanks, but suffered from inexperience compounded by hopelessly inadequate doctrine that left them tactically exposed to the veteran Panzer forces that opposed them. The lesson was an unforgiving one. (© CORBIS/Corbis via Getty Images)

of CCC led by Colonel Robert I. Stack, positioned by Hadjeb el Aïoun that lay 12 miles north of Djebel Lessouda. Fredendall was explicit in his orders: he expected an active defense that constantly probed the enemy's positions with aggressive patrolling, and that in the event of an attack the defenders were expected to hold their positions until the last man.

Under cover of night the four German *Kampfgruppen* assembled to the east of the Faïd and Maïzila passes. No artillery bombardment heralded the start of operations, the infantry elements of Kampfgruppe *Reimann* setting off at 0400hrs with motorized and armored elements following on an hour later. The coming dawn brought high winds and a sandstorm with it, obscuring the passes to the east and drowning out the sound of approaching armor. By 0600hrs Kampfgruppe *Reimann* and Kampfgruppe *Gerhardt* were well through the Faïd Pass, and it was only at around 0630hrs that the sandstorm cleared enough for Colonel Drake at his command post on Djebel Ksaira to make out two columns of Panzers in the act of encircling Djebel Lessouda, Kampfgruppe *Reimann* passing to the south and Kampfgruppe *Gerhardt* looping around from the north. Gerhardt's command had crashed into the small armored screening force at the foot of Lessouda and more or less annihilated it; the first American tank knocked out just happened to be the command vehicle and had the only radio, the rest following in quick succession, while the US infantry were overrun, with many of them killed in their foxholes by Panzers deliberately maneuvering on top of the entrenchments to collapse them and crush their occupants. Waters, still blinded by the dissipating sandstorm, was entirely unaware of the destruction of his covering force. He sent his staff officer to find out what was going on (never to see him again), but could soon enough make out for himself that the Germans were at his doorstep.

US artillery began firing on the entrance to the Faïd Pass, laying down barrages based on preplanned fire missions, but the *Kampfgruppen* were already well through by the time the firing started, the shells continuing to rain down on empty roads for the best part of an hour. Drake called for air support to no avail, Luftwaffe Ju 87 Stuka dive-bombers appearing instead at 0730hrs to begin a series of raids on Sidi Bou Zid that would continue throughout the day. By 0830hrs Djebel Lessouda was entirely encircled by Kampfgruppe *Gerhardt*, but the German force lacked the manpower to try for an assault on the hill, instead leaving a thin security cordon of troops from II./PzGrenRgt 86 around the hill's base, the rest of the group moving off toward Sidi Bou Zid.

Major Moore was unable to locate or contact Lieutenant Colonel Waters, and so found the defense of Djebel Lessouda falling entirely on his shoulders. Wary of mistakenly attacking American troops, Moore held back from engaging the forces in the valley, unsure of who they were, but as the morning wore on it became clear that several of the columns and patrols that were negotiating Djebel Lessouda's lower slopes were German, and he ordered them to be thrown back. Despite such skirmishing, no serious attack was launched on Djebel Lessouda, with Moore and his men little more than spectators to the rest of the battle developing in front of them.

The US artillery on the plain by Aïn Rebaou began to withdraw hurriedly to the west; B/91st AFAB, which had been supporting the American forces on Djebel Lessouda, was overrun, and a short while later Drake saw the first of 21. Panzer-Division's units, Kampfgruppe *Schütte*, approaching Sidi Bou

A PzKpfw VI Tiger heavy tank of 1./sPzAbt 501 in Tunisia, 1943. A total of 23 Tigers would serve throughout the Tunisian campaign (initially under the command of Major Hans-Georg Lueder until he was wounded in action on February 26, soon thereafter by Major August Seidensicker after the remnants of schwere Panzer-Abteilung 501 were merged with Seidensicker's newly arrived schwere Panzer-Abteilung 504 on March 17), all but three eventually being lost or captured. Nevertheless, their appearance in the German *Kampfgruppen* outside Sidi Bou Zid would prove to be a most unwelcome surprise for Hightower's US armored companies, whose job it was to blunt the attack. (AirSeaLand Photos)

John K. Waters

John Knight Waters was born in Baltimore on December 20, 1906. After spending two years at Johns Hopkins University he decided upon a career in military aviation, persuading a local politician to recommend him to West Point. His eyesight proved to be too poor for a pilot, so upon graduation in 1931 he instead went into the cavalry, during which time he met and married (then) Lieutenant Colonel George S. Patton's daughter Beatrice in 1934. By the time of the Allied landings in North Africa Waters had been given command of 1/1st Armored, taking part in the first tank battle between American and German forces at Chouigui Pass on November 26, 1942. During the German attack on Sidi Bou Zid, Waters was in command of Djebel Lessouda where, his position surrounded, he was captured by a German patrol, spending the rest of the war as a POW. After the war he was appointed commandant of cadets at West Point before going on to become Chief of Staff for I Corps in Korea in 1952, enjoying several increasingly prominent postings thereafter. He retired from the US Army in August 1966 with the rank of general, and died at the Walter Reed Army Medical Center on January 9, 1989.

Zid along Highway 83 from the southeast. The situation in the valley was increasingly precarious for the Americans, and by 0930hrs Hightower, at the head of his two companies of tanks and one of tank destroyers, sallied forth from Sidi Bou Zid in what he knew was little more than a delaying action. Within the hour his force was fully engaged 4 miles northeast of Sidi Bou Zid and suffering badly at the hands of 8.8cm shells from both Tiger tanks and antiaircraft guns. Hightower's M4 tanks and M3 GMCs fought furiously for over two hours, slowing the advance of the 10. Panzer-Division *Kampfgruppen* as he intended, but it was a losing battle; by midday his force of 47 tanks had been reduced to seven, Hightower and his crew among those who were forced to bail out of a burning M4 and escape the battlefield on foot, until they commandeered an abandoned half-track to make good their escape.

Colonel Drake, seeing the danger to his men on Djebel Ksaira if the enemy gained Djebel Garet Hadid, a spot of high ground 1 mile to the west of his position that flanked Highway 83, put together an impromptu battlegroup centered on his headquarters element, E/168th Infantry, a dragooned platoon of M3A1 light tanks, engineers of Company A, 16th Engineer Combat Battalion (a recent addition to his command that morning), and sundry stragglers pulled together from a variety of units. His force headed straight for Djebel Garet Hadid with the tank platoon in the lead, taking it by the skin of their teeth just before the Germans got there. Elements of Kampfgruppe *Schütte*'s Panzergrenadier-Regiment 104 launched a quick assault but were repulsed, after which they pulled back, surrounding Djebel Garet Hadid from all sides much as Gerhardt's men had done at Djebel Lessouda. Drake noted that though the initial attack had been knocked back, it would not have taken much for the Germans to break through; if Schütte's men had pressed the issue the small band of defenders could not have stopped them, but the initial repulse had been enough to buy the Americans some breathing space. In all around 950 US troops were on Djebel Garet Hadid, 300 of them unarmed, being men from tank, reconnaissance, artillery, and tank-destroyer units. Nearly 1,000 more – the majority of the 3/168th Infantry and some ad hoc supporting troops – remained on Djebel Ksaira under the command of Lieutenant Colonel John H. Van Vliet.

Rudolf Gerhardt

Rudolf Gerhardt was born in Greiz, Thuringia on March 26, 1896. Volunteering on the outbreak of World War I, he joined 7. Thüringisches Infanterie-Regiment 96 as a *Fahnenjunker*, serving on both the Eastern and Western fronts where he was wounded four times, won the Iron Cross First and Second Class, and rose to the rank of *Leutnant*, ending the war as the ordnance officer for his regiment. Rejoining the Heer in 1934, he was quickly detailed to the nascent Panzer-Regiment 1, his company leaving in 1936 to form the cadre of the new Panzer-Regiment 7 at Stuttgart-Vaihingen. Detached to command Panzer-Abteilung 66 in the Polish campaign, he saw much combat success (as well as being wounded again) before returning to his old unit in November as commander of II./PzRgt 7. Participating in Operation *Barbarossa*, he rose to command the regiment, being promoted to *Oberst* in April 1942. By year's end 10. Panzer-Division was committed to Tunisia where Gerhardt was again wounded in action on March 23, 1943, after which he joined Kesselring's staff before being given command of the Panzer-Lehr-Regiment. He fought against the Soviets in the Baltic theater before falling into American captivity on May 6, 1945. He died in Münster on November 10, 1964.

By midday McQuillin's HQ CCA had beaten a hasty retreat from Sidi Bou Zid, moving to the northwest so as to avoid encirclement; by 1500hrs the 2/17th FAR had attempted to redeploy to Highway 125 to the southwest of Sidi Bou Zid, but was destroyed by a mixture of concerted Axis air attacks and the approaching Panzers of Kampfgruppe *Stenkhoff*; and Kern spent the afternoon setting up a new forward defensive line at the crossroads that would soon bear his name. The US infantry on Djebel Lessouda, Djebel Ksaira, and Djebel Garet Hadid had no such options. Through several rounds of patchy radio calls Drake asked to withdraw from his obviously untenable position, but by 1410hrs his pleas had been refused – the request had gone from McQuillin to Ward and on to Fredendall the best part of 100 miles away, the answer coming back within ten minutes – Drake and his men were to stand firm, no matter what. Drake knew that he could hold out for some time, but not without help. Artillery and air attacks, punctuated by occasional ground sorties, maintained the pressure on the defenders, but none of the German assaults was large enough to overwhelm the Americans; the aim seemed to be to keep them hemmed in and their heads down. As the afternoon wore on Kampfgruppe *Stenkhoff* appeared from the southwest, the final pincer closing in on Sidi Bou Zid, already abandoned and bombed flat though it was. By early evening the spearheads of 21. Panzer-Division and 10. Panzer-Division connected to the west of the ruined town on Highway 125, sealing the day's victory.

For Drake, there was still some hope; he had gotten a messenger through to Ward's headquarters at Sbeïtla outlining the precariousness of his situation, and there was the expectation of a relief effort the following day. On Djebel Lessouda Waters had spent most of the battle cut off from all communication and unable to help direct the defense of his position in any way; soon enough his luck ran out and he was discovered by a German patrol who took him prisoner. Unable to establish communications with Waters, Drake, or Ward, Moore held his positions, though the fact that the Germans seemed to be ignoring him made things a little easier as night fell.

The following morning, February 15, brought an abrupt end to the rather eerie calm on Djebel Lessouda, the American positions coming under incessant shellfire throughout the day. The situation was much worse at Djebel Garet Hadid, where infantry assaults penetrated as far as the command post on three different occasions, with snipers and artillery taking a more or less constant toll on the defenders. There had been no food or water issued since the evening of February 13, and there were few medical supplies outside of basic first-aid kits to help minister to the increasing numbers of casualties. Drake's one chance was the prospect of relief by the 1st Armored Division, an effort which had been hastily organized around another armored battalion that had been rapidly drafted in to replace Hightower's destroyed unit.

Colonel Stack would command the counterattack, which would be spearheaded by Lieutenant Colonel James D. Alger's medium tanks of 2/1st Armored (the only reinforcement sent from Brigadier General Paul M. Robinett's CCB due to ongoing confusion at divisional and corps level over the larger strategic picture), with B/701st TDB as well as that battalion's reconnaissance company on the flanks for support. The force was rounded out by the 1st Armored Division's M3 half-track-equipped 3/6th Armored Infantry, as well as two batteries of 105mm T19 self-propelled howitzers from C/68th FAB. The battlegroup moved out at 1240hrs, having conducted no serious reconnaissance of the forces ahead of them, forces which they had been led to believe consisted of at most 40 to 60 Panzers. The German units, seeing the US advance, prepared an ambush; the American tanks would have to pass over several wadis on their approach, the deep and rock-strewn dry riverbeds only having a few places where they could be crossed easily, and it was at the last of these wadi-crossings that the German antitank guns had been focused. As expected, the M4 tanks and M3 half-tracks bunched up

A StuG III assault gun makes its way across a Tunisian plain in 1943, providing a lift for a squad of *Panzergrenadiere*. 10. Panzer-Division was one of the better-equipped units operating in North Africa, and had been expecting to add a full *Panzerjäger-Abteilung* to its establishment (as part of Panzer-Artillerie-Regiment 90), but in the end only a single battery of six StuG IIIs were transferred; all took part in the assault on Sidi Bou Zid. (AirSeaLand Photos)

at the choke points before fanning out into the open plain, whereupon the German antitank guns and 8.8cm antiaircraft guns opened up at 1540hrs, immediately destroying several vehicles. The Americans returned fire at once, only to find themselves attacked by strong Panzer forces on both flanks. By 1740hrs it was all over, with only four US tanks that had been held in reserve, most of the self-propelled artillery, and the 3/6th Armored Infantry surviving – the remaining 52 tanks of Alger's battalion were strewn across the plain, burning long into the night.

That evening on Djebel Lessouda Moore received an air-dropped message informing him that he was to take his battalion and break out, making for the American lines at Kern's Crossroads. Opting for boldness over subterfuge, at 2200hrs Moore had his men march out of their positions in two single files heading west, having destroyed all their equipment. The battalion made it over a mile before it came up against a challenge that could not be bluffed through, Moore giving the order his men had been briefed to expect – to scatter and run like hell. His gambit proved surprisingly successful, with 432 survivors – nearly half his battalion – eventually making it back to American lines over the following hours.

No such luck befell Drake and his men. The ferocious attacks that his positions had endured continued into the next day, February 16, the defenders on Djebel Ksaira and Djebel Garet Hadid being repeatedly battered by attack after attack, the lack of food and water coupled with dwindling reserves of ammunition exacerbating the mounting casualties, stress, and growing sense of despair. No relief came from the ground or the air, though at long last the order to attempt a withdrawal to Sbeïtla, initially given over the radio that afternoon, was confirmed by 2000hrs that evening. Preparations were already well underway in anticipation of the order to break out, with the wounded made as comfortable as possible and left in the care of medics, while every piece of equipment or weaponry that could be of use to the enemy was wrecked. Though Sbeïtla was their ultimate objective, Drake's force was much farther away than Moore's had been on Djebel Lessouda, and the high concentration of enemy forces meant that his men would try to make it to Djebel Hamra instead, thinking it was still in American hands.

The US evacuation began at 2200hrs on February 16, the 3/168th Infantry pulling out from Djebel Ksaira first, moving west and joining with the men of Drake's command from Djebel Garet Hadid on the long walk west. The column, only around 400 men strong – half of them lacking weapons – slipped through the patchy German cordon without much trouble and made good progress through the night, marching some 22–26 miles before daybreak, when their luck ran out. Spread out in the open, Drake's force encountered a motorized column that they initially thought was American but which all too quickly proved to be from one of the *Kampfgruppen*, the clatter of machine guns accompanying *Panzergrenadiere* leaping from their trucks. Drake fought his exhausted battlegroup as best he could for 3½ hours until it was completely encircled, finally being cut to pieces by a detachment of Panzers that had joined the German infantry for the kill. The ragged groups of Americans either surrendered or were shot down where they stood; Thomas Drake and the remnants of his command would spend the remainder of the war as prisoners.

The Kasserine Pass

February 19–20, 1943

BACKGROUND TO BATTLE

For the Americans the shock of defeat at Sidi Bou Zid caused Lieutenant-General Anderson to pull back from Gafsa in the face of anticipated German pressure, II Corps in effect drawing in its horns to what it assumed were more easily defensible central positions. Rommel's complement to Operation *Frühlingswind*, Operation *Morgenluft*, became redundant, with the focus of future maneuvers centered on exploiting the success German armor had already enjoyed at Sidi Bou Zid. Even so, the officer in command of 10. Panzer-Division and 21. Panzer-Division, Generalleutnant Heinz Ziegler, had moved cautiously in the wake of his victory despite his four

An American infantry unit marches through the Bahiret Foussana, the broad expanse of relatively flat ground that lay to the west of the Kasserine Pass, February–March 1943. Surrounded on all sides by mountains except for a small section to the northeast, it was incorrectly known as "Kasserine Valley" by the US forces that operated there. (Eliot Elisofon/The LIFE Picture Collection/Getty Images)

The crew of a 105mm M2 or M2A1 howitzer from B/33d FAB serve their gun, which is positioned in an Arabic mud-block structure, firing in defense of the Kasserine Pass, February 20, 1943. A US infantry division's artillery consisted of 48 guns divided between four battalions (each battalion had three four-gun batteries), one battalion of 155mm M1 howitzers tasked with general support and three battalions of 105mm M2 howitzers whose role was the direct support of the division's three infantry regiments. The main types of ammunition fired by the M2/M2A1 were the M1 high-explosive shell (33lb, max. range of 12,205yd at an elevation of 43.7°), the M67 HEAT shell (29.22lb, max. range 8,590yd), and M60 (FS) smoke shells (34.86lb, max. range 12,319yd). (Library of Congress)

Kampfgruppen having annihilated two American tank battalions and the best part of the 168th Infantry Regiment in relatively short order. He had inched forward with a timidity that infuriated Rommel but which met with Arnim's tacit approval, ever-conscious as he was of the daily cost in supplies and fuel demanded by offensive operations, and who still retained overall command of all the assets used in *Frühlingswind*. Sbeïtla was taken by the Germans on February 17, after which Armin, rather than driving on, left 21. Panzer-Division in place and pulled 10. Panzer-Division northeast, back toward the Fondouk and Pichon passes.

Rommel's first desire – to develop an attack toward the main supply base at Tébessa across the border in Algeria – remained unchanged, and he asked Kesselring to turn over Arnim's two *Panzer-Divisionen* to him so that he could continue on with the offensive, driving through the Kasserine Pass and then westward to the Algerian border. Such a move had the potential to destabilize the entire Allied presence in Tunisia and required yet more wrangling with the Comando Supremo in Rome, burning more time that the Germans could not afford to waste before the response eventually came: Rommel would indeed be given operational control of Arnim's battlegroup, but the objective was not to be Tébessa but a more modest tactical strike northward toward the town of Le Kef. It was less of a gamble, and if successful it would threaten the right flank of Anderson's First Army, but it also ran the risk of exposing the assaulting force's left flank as well as putting the German spearhead much closer to the center of a more easily reinforced Allied position. Knowing the likelihood of a possible change of heart from the Comando Supremo and aware, partly due to poor radio discipline among US radio operators, of the still-confused and brittle state of the American forces that lay to his front, Rommel opted to move as quickly as possible, advancing at once rather than spend more time concentrating his dispersed forces for a more focused thrust.

A German armored element made up of a PzKpfw III medium tank, an SdKfz 251 half-track armored personnel carrier, and accompanying *Kradschützen* (motorcycle riflemen) maneuver over rocky terrain toward a mountain range in Tunisia, 1943. The local environment around Kasserine proved itself hard on both the men and machines of Panzer and *Panzergrenadier* units, a situation exacerbated by the lack of spare parts and replacement vehicles arriving along the much-harried Axis supply lines. Nevertheless, the efficient and generally experienced German units that went to make up *Kampfgruppen* usually managed to adapt their tactics to both the terrain and the enemy that they were facing. (Bundesarchiv Bild 101I-788-0017-06 Foto: Dullin)

The new attack was to be known as Operation *Sturmflut* (Stormflood). In addition to the two Panzer divisions, Rommel had Kampfgruppe *DAK* commanded by Generalmajor Karl Bülowius as well as a motorized battlegroup from the Italian 131a Divisione Corazzata *Centauro*, both drawn from his now-defunct Deutsch-Italienische Panzerarmee. The operation was to begin at dawn on February 19: 21. Panzer-Division, still at Sbeïtla, was to attack north toward the Sbiba Gap, while Kampfgruppe *DAK* was to try to force its way through the Kasserine Pass. Still up at Fondouk and Pichon, 10. Panzer-Division was to head south to Sbeïtla, whereupon it could reinforce whichever thrust – the Sbiba Gap or Kasserine – had been the most successful. The *Centauro* battlegroup was to attack farther to the south, through the Dernaïa Pass. For once, Rommel seemed intent on obeying his orders to make Le Kef his objective, in spite of the greater glory offered by a strike at Tébessa.

Kampfgruppe *DAK* consisted of Aufklärungs-Abteilung (mot.) 3 (Major Hans von Luck), Panzergrenadier-Regiment *Afrika* (Oberst Otto Menton), I./PzRgt 8 (Major Hans-Günter Stotten), an 8.8cm-equipped *Flakkampftruppe*, and Werfer-Regiment 71. Arnim, out of necessity or spite, refused to release all of 10. Panzer-Division to Rommel, keeping a portion of the unit's Panzers as well as the Tigers of schwere Panzer-Abteilung 501 for his own use. The resulting force was called Kampfgruppe *von Broich* after its leader, the commander of 10. Panzer-Division Generalmajor Friedrich Freiherr von Broich, and included I./PzRgt 7, Panzergrenadier-Regiment 86, Panzergrenadier-Regiment 69, Panzer-Aufklärungs-Abteilung 10, Panzerjäger-Abteilung 90, and Kradschützen-Bataillon 10. The *Centauro* battlegroup (Generale Giorgio Carlo Calvi di Bergolo) was made up of the 5o Reggimento bersaglieri with supporting armored elements from 31o Reggimento carri.

The American dispositions were still suffering from being dispersed over a significant portion of the Eastern Dorsal, a situation exacerbated by the pell-mell retreat occasioned by the calamitous defense of Sidi Bou Zid. Major General Ward's 1st Armored Division had pulled back to the environs of Tébessa to provide protection to the town as well as to give the unit a chance to catch its breath after the disasters of the last few days, while Brigadier General Robinett's CCB had retreated to the Algerian border to guard the approaches to Tébessa. The American retreat necessitated the establishment of covering forces to ensure the security of the routes of withdrawal, one of the most important being through the Kasserine Pass. Colonel Anderson T.W. Moore, commanding the 19th Engineer Regiment, was detailed to assist in covering the retreat of the 1st Armored Division and its associated elements by deploying the 1,200 men under his command to block any potential access to the Kasserine Pass by the Axis forces.

During February 16, Moore had his men lay 3,000 mines along either side of the road that led from Kasserine to the pass, but had achieved little else in the way of defensive preparation; much of their barbed-wire allotment, rather than being placed to obstruct obvious enemy approaches, was still on its spools. The following day they established a 3-mile-wide defensive line a little way behind the mouth of the pass (the idea being that any attacker would have to funnel through the 800yd-wide "choke point" to engage Moore's position), with three engineer companies established either side of the Hatab River and one engineer company in reserve. Moore's men were good enough at building roads, but they were inexperienced soldiers who had not even completed their rifle training before being sent overseas; only one of them had ever seen any sort of action before (Atkinson 2002: 368).

A PzKpfw IV Ausf F2 medium tank parked at the Kasserine Pass near the crew's tent, while two tank drivers consult a map, February 1943. The turret marking "514" indicated that the tank was from 5. Panzer-Kompanie, 1. Panzer-Zug, vehicle number 4, most likely from 10. Panzer-Division's Panzer-Regiment 7. (Heinrich Hoffmann/ Mondadori Portfolio via Getty Images)

The Kasserine Pass, February 19–20, 1943

1 0730hrs, February 19: Colonel Alexander N. Stark arrives to take up his new command, just as the attack by Major Hans von Luck's Aufklärungs-Abteilung (mot.) 3 is thwarted by artillery and machine-gun fire.

2 1030hrs, February 19: II./PzGrenRgt *Afrika* launches an attack toward Djebel Semmama while its I./PzGrenRgt *Afrika* strikes toward Djebel Chambi. Initially, both battalions have a degree of success, but their attacks eventually falter.

3 *c.*1300hrs–1730hrs, February 19: Three companies of US reinforcements from the 3/39th Infantry (9th Infantry Division) arrive throughout the afternoon and are sent into the line.

4 0400hrs, February 20: Gore Force and the 3/6th Armored Infantry take up position on the Thala road and the reverse slope of Djebel Semmama to prevent potential German breakthroughs.

5 0830hrs, February 20: The German attack recommences, preceded by a massive artillery bombardment including *Nebelwerfern*. By 1200hrs the right flank of the American line, manned by the 19th Engineer Regiment, fractures under constant German pressure.

6 1630hrs, February 20: The final German attack, augmented by units from 10. Panzer-Division, breaks through to the north and south. Gore Force is destroyed and all American positions at the mouth of the pass are overrun.

Battlefield environment

The Kasserine Pass offered a way through the Eastern Dorsal mountain range that gave out into a broad basin of relatively flat ground known as the Bahiret Foussana. The bottom of the pass was bisected by the Hatab River, its course roughly followed by a road that split at the mouth of the pass, the western spur heading toward Tébessa and Haïdra and the eastern spur to Thala. The mouth of the pass was also bisected by the Gafsa–Sbeïtla rail line that ran north through the pass up to Haïdra. For a defender the open base of the pass would be difficult to defend without proper emplacements; the obvious option was to concentrate on the point of the pass where the road,

river, and rail lines converged between the closest outcrops of the flanking hills. Even with the funneling effect the pass was still over 800yd wide at its narrowest point, with the Hatab River (in full flow at this time of year) effectively cutting any defensive position into two separate forces on the river's right and left banks. The flanking ridgelines of Djebel Semmama (4,447ft) to the northeast and Djebel Chambi (5,064ft) to the southwest offered good vantage points overlooking the pass and its approaches, their rocky terrain making them safe from mechanized assault but difficult to adapt into strong defensive positions.

A view of the landscape of the Kasserine Pass taken around the time of the battle. The difficult nature of the landscape is immediately apparent. Djebel Semmama and Djebel Chambi, the hills that flanked the road and which would host some of the troops of the 1/26th Infantry in their defense of the pass, were mostly inaccessible to armor and difficult terrain for infantry as well, being riven with gullies and patches of dead ground and covered with loose rock, all of which offered many advantages for an intelligent defender. (Dmitri Kessel/The LIFE Picture Collection/Getty Images)

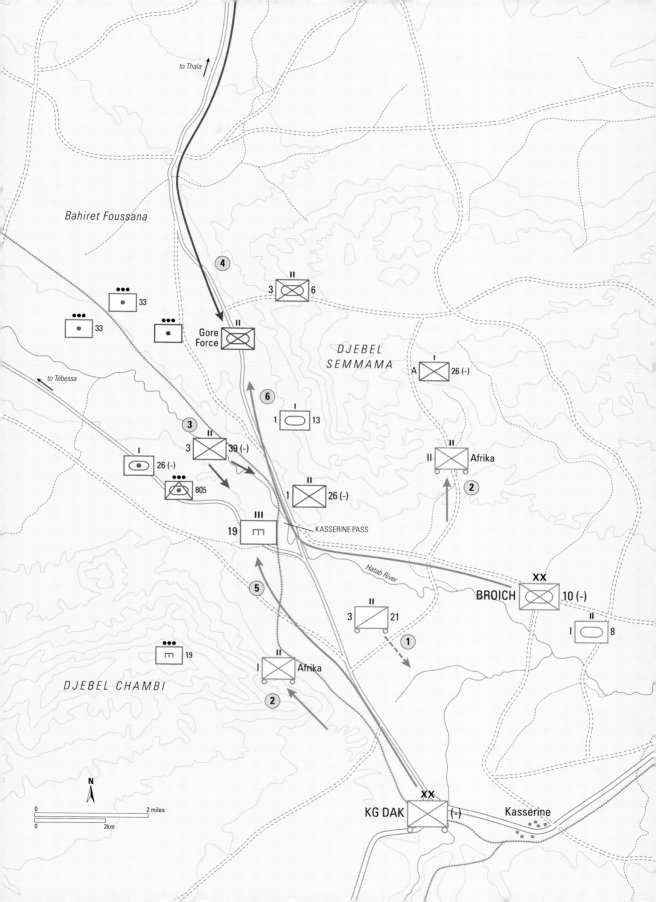

to Thala ↑

Bahiret Foussana

④

II
3 ⊠ 6

•••• 33

•••• 33

•••• Gore
Force II
⊠

DJEBEL
SEMMAMA

I
A ⊠ 26 (-)

to Tébessa

⑥

I
1 ⬭ 13

③
II
3 ⊠ 39 (-)

II
II ⊠ Afrika

②

I
•• 26 (-)

•••• ⬭ 805

II
1 ⊠ 26 (-)

III
19 ⊞

KASSERINE PASS

XX
BROICH ⊠ 10 (-)

•••• ⊞ 19

DJEBEL CHAMBI

Hatab River

II
3 ⊠ 21

①

I
I ⬭ 8

II
I ⊠ Afrika

⑤

②

N

0 ———————— 2 miles
0 ———————— 2km

XX
KG DAK ⊠ (-)   Kasserine

INTO COMBAT

Some 800 men of Lieutenant Colonel Gerald C. Kelleher's 1/26th Infantry arrived to support Moore's force, taking up positions in the center of the pass floor on the north side of the Hatab River blocking the Thala road, with one platoon from A/26th Infantry establishing itself on the slopes of Djebel Semmama. To the 1/26th Infantry's right on the other side of the Hatab River were now all three companies of engineers blocking the Tébessa road (one platoon positioned on the slopes of Djebel Chambi), with the fourth company still positioned behind them as a reserve. Additional support was provided by I/13th Armored (eight M4 tanks) and some M3 GMCs of the 805th Tank Destroyer Battalion, placed in the center of Bahiret Foussana. Artillery support was provided by two 105mm M2 howitzer batteries (eight guns) from the 33d Field Artillery Battalion, the 26th Infantry Regiment's Cannon Company (four 75mm T30 HMCs), and a French battery (four venerable horse-drawn 75mm guns). Farther back to the west there was Robinett's CCB, while Brigadier Charles A.L. Dunphie and his British 26th Armored Brigade were placed at Thala a little over 20 miles away from the mouth of the pass so that he would be able to reinforce American positions at either Sbiba or Kasserine as required.

During the night of February 18/19, Colonel Alexander N. Stark, commanding officer 26th Infantry Regiment, was informed that he was now in charge of the Kasserine defenses. On a cold morning, the sky overcast and the ground still wet from the night's rain, Stark arrived at 0730hrs to find his new command already going into action. He immediately detailed another platoon from A/26th Infantry to Djebel Semmama to reinforce the valley shoulders, while doing the same with the engineers on the other side of the pass. It would be nigh on impossible for Stark to reorganize his defensive line as the Hatab River made passage from the north side of the pass to the south side extremely difficult, especially under enemy fire. Mostly dry during the summer, in February the river was in full flow, the only bridge being 5 miles back in the Bahiret Foussana. Stark would have to fight his 2,000-strong force from the positions they currently occupied.

Major Hans von Luck of Aufklärungs-Abteilung (mot.) 3 was tasked with taking the pass by a *coup de main*, seizing it and holding it open for supporting units to follow on through. With his *Kradschützen* in the vanguard, Luck's force moved off at around 0630hrs, advancing down the rain-soaked roadway without artillery preparation in the hope of catching the defenders unawares, but the fire from the French 75s that began straddling his column quickly disabused Luck of that notion; machine-gun fire joined the artillery barrage, forcing his troops to seek cover. It seemed to Luck that the hills either side of the pass were peppered with alert men and efficient artillery forward observers. With the element of surprise long gone and his unit unable to progress farther, Luck pulled his men back to the relative safety of the foothills around Djebel Chambi southwest of the pass (Luck 2002: 142).

Bülowius then sent forward Menton's Panzergrenadier-Regiment *Afrika*. II./PzGrenRgt *Afrika* was ordered to make an assault on the slopes of Djebel Semmama, which were fairly shallow when approached from the east, supported by fire from Kampfgruppe *DAK*'s artillery and a battery of

8.8cm antiaircraft guns. At around the same time I./PzGrenRgt *Afrika* was committed to an assault on the other side of the valley, moving around the base of Djebel Chambi and into the throat of the pass. At 1015hrs the regiment's 35–40 trucks drove to within striking distance of the hills, whereupon both *Panzergrenadier* battalions disembarked and moved out. At Djebel Semmama the *Panzergrenadiere* had a degree of success, some men advancing along the valley floor and others up the hill's lower reaches, taking a prominent knoll on the hillside, but constant rifle and machine-gun fire from the defenders supported by artillery fire meant that the advance bogged down. On the southern side the German attack along the base of Djebel Chambi went well enough until Menton's *Panzergrenadiere* ran into a barrage from the 33d Field Artillery Battalion, which forced them back. The poor weather resulted in a lack of close air support that, when coupled with ineffective counterbattery fire from the Germans' own guns, further reduced the effectiveness of both attacks (Howe 1957: 449).

By early afternoon some much-needed US reinforcements began to appear; three companies from the 3/39th Infantry (9th Infantry Division) were sent forward as soon as they arrived. I/39th Infantry was ordered to the center of the pass to bolster the left flank of Moore's engineer companies (all four of which were now committed); L/39th Infantry reinforced the two platoons from A/26th Infantry on Djebel Semmama; and K/39th Infantry was split, one half going to the right flank of Moore's engineers and the other being sent to support B/26th and C/26th Infantry on the American left. Stark further reinforced his left flank, moving five M4 tanks from I/13th Armored along the Thala road to protect against any German incursions, with the other three tanks plus the M3 GMCs of the 805th Tank Destroyer Battalion and the four guns of the 26th Infantry Regiment's Cannon Company sent to perform the same function to the right on the Tébessa road. During a brief visit, Dunphie found Stark calm in the face of what the British officer thought was an extremely tenuous situation, Stark having no real reserves other than his small armored stopgaps on his flanks. In addition, Dunphie was very concerned about enemy infiltration, of which there were already some strong indications.

A column of Italian Semovente M41 75/18 self-propelled guns from the *Centauro* Division pictured on February 16, 1943, just prior to their engagement in the upcoming Kasserine battles. Generally regarded as the best Italian armored vehicle of the war, the Semovente M41 75/18 was armed with the 75mm Obice da 75/18 modello 34 mountain gun set on an M14/41 chassis. (AirSeaLand Photos)

The fight for Djebel Semmama

US view: The morning of February 19 – damp, overcast, and windy – has seen an attack develop against the American forces defending the Kasserine Pass. After an initial German reconnaissance probe is repulsed, a much more significant assault is launched around 1030hrs by a battalion of soldiers from Panzergrenadier-Regiment *Afrika*, their objective being to advance on the foothills of Djebel Semmama on the eastern side of the Kasserine Pass, defended by the 1/26th Infantry. The rough and rocky ground is sodden from days of rain, but it still proves resistant to the digging of effective entrenchments, so the American infantry are having to make the most of the natural cover provided by the rugged terrain. The members of this rifle squad have pulled back from their initial prepared positions to escape the worst of the increasingly intense German artillery fire, and are now holding a ridgeline on the western slopes of Djebel Semmama that overlooks the Kasserine–Thala road winding its way northwestward through the pass. A BAR gunner lies prone, going through magazine after magazine firing at the advancing Germans, supported by the rifles of his squad-mates around him. Several men who were hit earlier by bullets and shell splinters have been dragged to one side until they can be evacuated – another man lies dead, slumped below the ridge. Crouching behind the firing line, the platoon lieutenant is in a rushed discussion with his staff sergeant about how best to redeploy the men in their new position.

German view: A brazen German attempt to force a passage through the Kasserine Pass having failed, the soldiers of Panzergrenadier Regiment *Afrika* have been committed to battle, their job to sweep resistance from the Kasserine–Thala road and drive the Americans off the slopes of Djebel Semmama that lies to the north of the road, dominating its passage into the Foussana basin. The German soldiers soon find Djebel Semmama's scrubby and rock-covered foothills are treacherous and difficult to navigate, a situation made much worse by the surprising stubbornness of American resistance. The gunnery and small-arms fire is taking its toll on the attackers as they make their way through the rough terrain, with more than a few men already having fallen wounded or dead. The Germans move as fast as they can using whatever cover is available among the rocky ground, but the increasing difficulty of the advance drives the *Leutnant* and his much-reduced platoon into the temporary shelter provided by a shallow defile. He bellows an order to the MG 34 team to hurry forward and bring their gun into action so he can try to suppress the hail of gunfire coming from the slopes a few hundred yards to his front; while the gun crew dash toward a spot to set up their LMG, the rest of his men follow the instructions of their *Feldwebel* and scramble for cover or a good vantage point, some of them returning fire as best they can.

The slow progress of his *Panzergrenadiere* forced Bülowius to commit I./PzRgt 8 as part of another offensive at around 1540hrs. The Panzers, attacking with infantry and artillery support along the southern edge of Djebel Chambi, ran into some haphazardly placed mines which knocked out five of them, while others became bogged down. The battle on the hills themselves had continued throughout the day, with the Germans making fitful progress. To hurry things along two companies of *Panzergrenadiere*, one on Djebel Semmama and the other on Djebel Chambi, were tasked with scaling the more inaccessible routes to the summit, routes that were difficult for the defenders to see or take under fire. Led by Oberleutnant Schmidt and Oberleutnant Bucholz, many of the men of the two companies had originally been in the *Gebirgsjäger-Kompanie* when their unit was still known as Sonderverband 288, chosen for their skill in operating in mountainous terrain. As the evening wore on, groups of *Panzergrenadiere* gained the heights on both sides of the pass, using the cover of darkness to move among the American positions, attacking and overwhelming isolated pockets of troops. The two US platoons on Djebel Semmama were effectively cut off, while in all around 100 soldiers were taken prisoner, men Stark could ill-afford to lose.

The situation on the valley floor was also becoming increasingly serious for the Americans. Morale among the engineer companies on the right of the line was low, the men having endured a day of serious fighting. More than a few of Moore's engineers had abandoned their positions as the evening wore on, victims of what was sometimes called "night fever," a state where physical discomfort and fear blend to break the resolve of a man to stay and fight (Blumenson 1967: 241). The situation got so bad an entire company broke and ran when their supporting tank destroyers moved unexpectedly. The two batteries of 105mm guns from the 33d Field Artillery Battalion had also pulled back – without orders – leaving the French battery of four horse-drawn 75s to serve as Stark's sole artillery support (Atkinson 2002: 372). The US left flank was also under severe pressure, with the waves of German attacks battering the line held by the two companies of the 1/26th Infantry to such an extent that by 2030hrs the battalion command post had been reported overrun. The company on Djebel Semmama was surrounded during the night, and the remaining companies were out of battalion control, fighting their own battles without recourse to higher command.

Stark's position was under immense strain; though the men on both his flanks were still holding, they had no significant reinforcements on the way. The crests of both hills were being contested, and German infiltration maneuvers on the floor of the pass threatened to encircle both flanks. Stark gave orders that if such an event came about, the surrounded units should attempt to break out and head for the slopes of the nearest hill where they could re-establish their defense, a desperate idea that revealed the extremity of the situation. The Germans kept close contact throughout the night, with aggressive patrols ensuring that there was no let-up in the pressure being applied to all parts of the American line.

As the new day dawned the weather continued dull and foggy, with rain throughout the night having kept the ground sodden. A British combined-arms unit drawn from Dunphie's brigade, known as "Gore Force" after its commander, Lieutenant-Colonel Adrian C. Gore, was stationed on the Thala road near the northwest corner of the Bahiret Foussana. It comprised seven Valentine infantry tanks and four Crusader cruiser tanks of C Squadron, 2nd Lothians and Border Horse, along with a company of motorized infantry and a battery of artillery. Arriving early in the morning of February 20, the 3/6th Armored Infantry under the command of Lieutenant Colonel W.W. Wells was detailed by Stark to support Gore Force's flank rather than reinforce his own forward position (Zaloga 2005: 58).

The new day had started with another round of German attacks led by Panzergrenadier-Regiment *Afrika*, jumping off at 0830hrs and supported by a bombardment involving all of Kampfgruppe *DAK*'s guns and including some salvoes by the 21cm "Screaming Meemie" rockets of Werfer-Regiment 71. Although the German spearheads failed to make headway on either side of the pass, the assault wore the already threadbare nerves of the Allied soldiers on the front line even thinner as Bülowius continued to press his simultaneous attacks along the Thala and Tébessa roads. Gore Force, supported by Wells' 3/6th Armored Infantry, who had parked their M3 half-tracks at the base of Djebel Semmama before scaling its slopes, opposed the attack developing along the Thala road. Though there seemed to be more Axis success to the south, where a battalion from the newly arrived 5o Reggimento bersaglieri supported the advance of I./PzGrenRgt *Afrika* at Djebel Chambi, effective American artillery and mortar fire slowed things down considerably.

By mid-morning Rommel had arrived at the battlefield and was less than pleased to find that Bülowius was yet to secure the pass. His other option, the advance of 21. Panzer-Division toward the Sbiba Gap, had proved to be a much tougher nut to crack than the Germans had anticipated, so much so that Rommel was now determined to throw the full weight of his force at Kasserine to ensure a breakthrough. Meeting with Bülowius and Broich near the pass, Rommel ordered a new assault as soon as Broich's 10. Panzer-Division – still slogging its way through the Tunisian mud on the road from Sbeïtla – finally arrived. In anticipation of moving against Kasserine, Rommel had ordered the 5o Reggimento bersaglieri (already in action) and a battalion of 75mm Semovente da 75/18 self-propelled guns from 31o Reggimento carri to make for the pass. This new force, in conjunction with Kampfgruppe *DAK* and 10. Panzer-Division, would launch a major blow if the ragged American lines defending the valley floor and the adjacent hills were still holding out.

Even before that new German offensive had time to develop, the situation among the American positions was starting to unravel. The right flank, still held by the engineers, was pierced by an armored column, with the Panzers beginning to find their way through the minefield. The French 75s, finally out of ammunition, were spiked, their gunners retreating to safety. Moore radioed Stark at noon, telling him that the 19th Engineer Regiment command post was being overrun and that he was moving to set up a new post, but that was almost immediately cut up by machine-gun fire and quickly overrun in turn, Moore and one other officer managing to escape and make it back to Stark's headquarters around an hour later. The engineer companies disintegrated, pulling out as and when they could, making their way as individuals or small

groups back across the Bahiret Foussana; any coherent defense of the Tébessa road was all but over.

The Allied defense was evaporating, though the reality of the situation was not clear to the Germans. As the afternoon progressed the leading elements of 10. Panzer-Division started arriving, and 1630hrs saw the launch of Rommel's coordinated assault on the pass, the newly strengthened *Angriffsgruppen* punching through the Tébessa and Thala roads. Gore Force put up stiff resistance, forcing Bülowius to commit I./PzRgt 8 after which the British armor was all but wiped out, the German thrust along the Thala road also cutting off the trapped remnants of A/26th Infantry together with the 3/6th Armored Infantry, marooned on Djebel Semmama. I/13th Armored lost one platoon, also cut off on Djebel Semmama, while the majority of the 3/6th Armored Infantry's M3 armored personnel carriers were captured intact by the Germans. As the night began to close in, Stark abandoned his headquarters, which was in imminent danger of being overrun. His journey back to Dunphie's headquarters was fraught and difficult, and he came close to being captured or killed more than once.

The Kasserine Pass had fallen and in theory opened the way for a German advance toward El Kef or Tébessa. The bridge over the Hatab River having been blown by US engineers, there was no easy way for Rommel to consolidate his forces, so he did not do so, instead sending Kampfgruppe *DAK* toward Tébessa and 10. Panzer-Division northward to Thala, while 21. Panzer-Division continued to knock at the door of the Sbiba Gap. This dissipation meant that no Axis force was strong enough to overcome its local opposition – an opposition that, unlike the German effort, was growing stronger with each passing hour. With time and logistics against him, Rommel acknowledged that he could not exploit the success at Kasserine. The German withdrawal order went out at 1415hrs on February 22. Within a day, the majority of Axis units were clear of the Kasserine Pass, wrong-footing the Allies once again, who took several days to realize that Rommel had pulled back from the pass in earnest.

ABOVE RIGHT
German artillerymen in the process of firing their 15cm schwere Feldhaubitze 18 (sFH 18) heavy howitzer during the Tunisian campaign, January–February 1943. With a crew of nine men to operate it, the sFH 18 fired a 43.52kg (95.95lb) high-explosive shell out to a maximum range of 13,325m (14,572yd). A standard 1939 *Infanterie-Division* had an integral *Artillerie-Regiment* that included one battalion of 12 sFH 18 pieces (three *Batterien* of four guns each), while for a *Panzer-Division* the third *Batterie* would be equipped with four 10.5cm schwere Kanone 18 heavy field guns instead. (Bundesarchiv Bild 101I-554-0865-17A Foto: Stocker, Dr.)

El Guettar

March 23, 1943

BACKGROUND TO BATTLE

By March 9 Rommel was gone, sent back to Germany in a state of exhaustion. Promoted to replace Rommel, Arnim still had to consult Kesselring and gain the Comando Supremo's approval for significant moves, but the arguments over how best to engage the enemy were over. The spirit of reorganization had also spread to the Allies. Fredendall's failings having been exposed by II Corps' haphazard performance, General Dwight D. Eisenhower, the Supreme Allied Commander in the Mediterranean Theater of Operations, replaced him with Major General George S. Patton on March 6.

On February 27, the 1st Infantry Division left the front line for ten days' rest at Marsott, northwest of Tébessa, where it drew together all its organic elements for the first time in the campaign. When Allen's command headed for the Italian-held town of Gafsa, the move was part of a new limited offensive ordered by General Sir Harold R.L.G. Alexander, commander of the 18th Army Group, formed on February 20 to rationalize coordination between the First and Eighth armies. II Corps was to advance on Gafsa, secure

it, and establish a supply dump there, ensuring the security of Montgomery's left flank as his Eighth Army attempted to penetrate the Mareth Line and move up the coastal plain.

Patton ordered Allen to advance on Gafsa on March 17. The Italian and German defenders of Gafsa pulled out, leaving Allen to take the town without a shot being fired. The unexpected speed of II Corps' success, coupled with the impending launch of Operation *Pugilist*, Montgomery's attack at Mareth that was set to commence on March 19, gave Patton another chance to bring his forces into action. The plan called for an advance along two axes. The first, centered on Ward's 1st Armored Division, would take Sened Station and then continue to Maknassy. The second would see Allen's 1st Infantry Division and supporting elements move east along the Gafsa–Gabès road through El Guettar, captured on March 18 by Lieutenant Colonel William O. Darby's 1st Ranger Battalion, and into the plains beyond.

Darby's Rangers acted as the vanguard for Allen's division. Setting off on the evening of March 20, the 500 men of the 1st Ranger Battalion and a 70-strong supporting mortar unit moved down the Gafsa–Gabès road before making their way through the mountainous terrain that lay to the north of the route. As dawn broke on March 21 they appeared on the high ground overlooking the main Italian position defending the Gumtree Road, their surprise attack routing the enemy and bagging over 1,000 prisoners. Allen now moved through El Guettar and into the hills to the east, flanking the Gumtree and Gafsa–Gabès roads. The US position spread out into a loose chain that ran across the road, the wings anchored along the high ground that made up the sides of the valley. The same day saw Sened Station fall to Ward's forces, though his progress was slowed by the muddy Tunisian roads.

Fighting along the Mareth Line was well underway, and though Montgomery had not yet broken through, the Germans were concerned at the prospect of American divisions arriving in their right rear. Determined to neutralize the threat posed by the American battlegroups, Arnim instructed 10. Panzer-Division to move from the coast, its orders to interdict and throw back II Corps' advance at Maknassy and El Guettar.

Three American soldiers of the Tank Destroyer Force (from left: Privates Thurman Reltor, Leon Jeannotte, and Chelsea Bate) take cover during a German bombing attack in the El Guettar valley, 1943. They have made the most of the natural cover that such rugged terrain could occasionally provide, though the ground often proved too rocky to dig proper foxholes, American soldiers instead having to build up impromptu sangars of loose scree for protection. The tank destroyers, though vulnerable, would play an important role at El Guettar. (Eliot Elisofon/ The LIFE Picture Collection/ Getty Images)

1 **0700hrs:** 10. Panzer-Division advances toward US positions in the El Guettar valley. The force splits into three separate *Angriffsgruppen* (attacking groups) that attack toward the hills to the north and south, as well as the El Keddab ridge in the center which blocks access from the valley to the town.

2 **0700hrs:** Two companies from II./PzGrenRgt 69 launch an attack on Hill 482, defended by K/18th Infantry. The rough terrain and fierce resistance mean the attack bogs down for the rest of the day.

3 **0730hrs:** The main German attack hits the 3/18th Infantry near Hill 336. The US position is overrun. A force of Panzers moves down the road toward El Guettar until its progress is interrupted by M3 GMCs of the 601st Tank Destroyer Battalion. A mix of bad ground, mines, artillery, and fire from the M3 GMCs stall the Panzers' advance.

4 ***c.*0900hrs:** The 32d and 5th Field Artillery battalions are overrun, spiking their guns and retreating.

5 ***c.*0950hrs:** M10 GMCs of the 899th Tank Destroyer Battalion arrive to reinforce the 601st Tank Destroyer Battalion but are roughly handled by the more experienced Panzer forces they encounter.

6 ***c.*1300hrs:** German forces withdraw, allowing both sides to regroup.

7 **1645hrs:** The second major German attack of the day begins, led by a large armored force supported by infantry: Hill 336 and the 3/18th Infantry are once more the focus of the German assault. Despite some penetration of American positions, by *c.*1740hrs the Germans have been thrown into disarray by accurate artillery fire, calling off their attack and retreating from the valley.

Battlefield environment

From Gafsa two roads led east to the coastal towns of Sfax and Gabès, passing through narrow plains separated by a central spur of mountainous territory. The more northerly route led to the pass at Maknassy and from there to Sfax, while the southerly route was a macadam-topped road that passed through the town of El Guettar and on to Gabès. To the east of the small oasis town of El Guettar the Gabès road forked, the left-hand spur known as the Gumtree Road running north around a large area of high ground that dominated access through the valley. To the south of the Gabès road the long narrow plain of the valley floor gave way to the dominating slopes of Djebel Berda and the smaller outcropping of Djebel Kreroua. Once off the road the valley offered fairly rough passage over ground that was rocky and uneven, with a complicated mix of heights, ridgelines, ravines, and gullies defining the uneven hills that flanked its passage. Finally, toward the western edge of the valley on the southern side of the road lay the Chott El Guettar, a broad sandy area that was impassable for most vehicles, especially tracked armor.

A wrecked PzKpfw IV sits on the plain after the battle of El Guettar, April 1, 1943. The stark contrast between the relatively flat grass and scrubland of the valley floor and the mountainous backdrop is plain to see, though even flat ground could be treacherous, cut through with twisting wadis and often littered with loose rock. Operating successfully in such an environment demanded a strong understanding of the advantages and pitfalls of local terrain, as well as a practical combined-arms doctrine. (Eliot Elisofon/The LIFE Picture Collection/Getty Images)

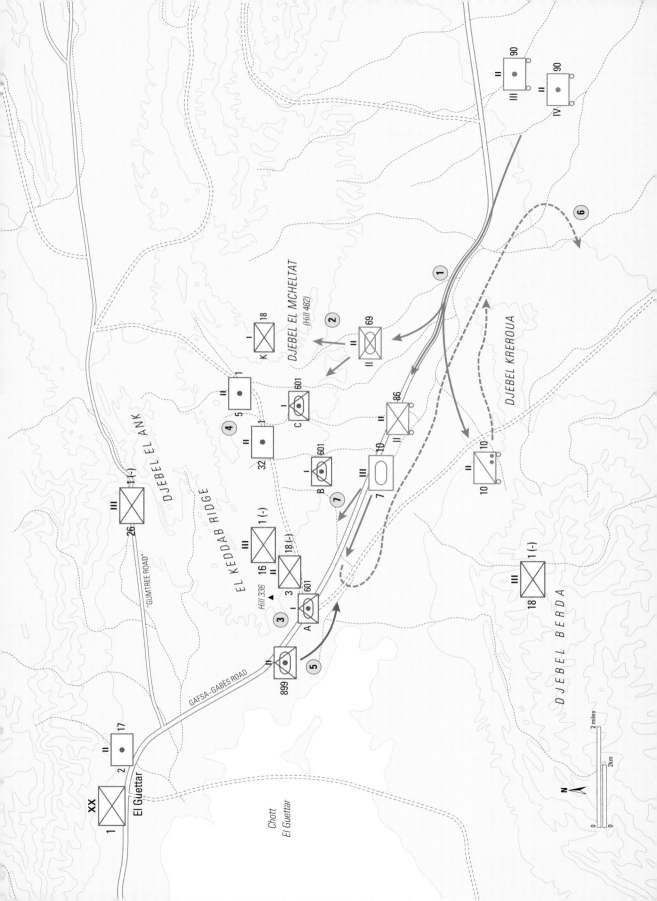

INTO COMBAT

Forewarned of a potential German attack by intelligence reports, Allen stopped his advance and dug his division in across the broad basin of the valley around 8 miles to the east of the town of El Guettar. Allen's infantry assets included Colonel d'Alary Fechet's 16th Infantry Regiment (less 1/16th Infantry), the 18th Infantry Regiment (Colonel Frank U. Greer), the 26th Infantry Regiment (Colonel Alexander N. Stark), and the 1st Ranger Battalion (Lieutenant Colonel William O. Darby). These foot soldiers were deployed alongside the M3 GMC-equipped 601st Tank Destroyer Battalion (31 75mm M3 GMCs and five 37mm M6 GMCs; Lieutenant Colonel Herschel D. Baker); the M10 GMCs of the 899th Tank Destroyer Battalion (Lieutenant Colonel Maxwell A. Tincher) were in reserve at Gafsa a little over 13 miles away, while artillery support came from the 2/17th FAR (most of the battalion temporarily equipped with 105mm guns after it lost many of its 155mm pieces at Sidi Bou Zid) and the 5th (155mm; Major Robert N. Tyson) and 32d (105mm; Lieutenant Colonel Percy W. Thompson) Field Artillery battalions. The 26th Infantry Regiment was positioned on the Gumtree Road to the north of Hill 621, protecting the left flank. The 16th Infantry Regiment (less the 2/16th Infantry in reserve at El Guettar and the 3/16th Infantry garrisoning Gafsa) was stationed in the center together with the 3/18th Infantry along the El Keddab Ridge, a rise of rough ground that ran roughly from north to south across the valley basin, and which had a knoll of high ground toward its southern edge that overlooked the road, Hill 336. The remaining two battalions, the 1/18th and 2/18th Infantry, had been detailed to the rugged heights of Djebel Berda across the road to the south. The companies of the 601st Tank Destroyer Battalion were positioned to the north of the Gafsa–Gabès road, with A/601st TDB on a hillside overlooking the northern edge of the road and B/601st TDB and C/601st TDB in front of the divisional artillery positions that lay to the south of Djebel el Ank.

By the evening of March 22, 10. Panzer-Division's dash from the coast had brought the German tanks to within 10 miles of the American positions at El Guettar. Led by Generalmajor Friedrich Freiherr von Broich and totaling around 6,000 men, the division's *Kampfgruppe* consisted of Oberst Rudolf Gerhardt's Panzer-Regiment 7 (two battalions, totaling around 50 PzKpfw III and PzKpfw IV medium tanks), II./PzGrenRgt 69 (Major Paul Pomée), II./PzGrenRgt 86 (Hauptmann Wilhelm Leyendecker), Stabs-Kompanie/PzGrenRgt 86 (Oberst Hans Reimann), Kradschützen-Bataillon 10 (Major Dr. Heinrich Drewes), Panzer-Pionier-Bataillon 49 (Major Albert Krumsiek), one company from Panzerjäger-Abteilung 90 (seven StuG III assault guns), Major Alfred von Rosenberg-Lipinsky's III./PzArtRgt 90 (10.5cm leFH 18), the antiaircraft guns of IV./PzArtRgt 90 (Major Dr Montada), and a detachment from 131a Divisione Corazzata *Centauro*. The remaining elements of 10. Panzer-Division, including both remaining *Panzergrenadier* battalions and the Tigers of schwere Panzer-Abteilung 501 (now augmented by the newly arrived schwere Panzer-Abteilung 504) had been grouped into Kampfgruppe *Lang* and were to the north at the Maknassy Pass.

At 0300hrs on March 23 the German division, its engines thundering into life, began to make its way west toward Allen's position. The first

indications of German intentions came in to the 1st Infantry Division's headquarters at 0430hrs, reports of activity that were soon confirmed by elements of the 601st Tank Destroyer Battalion who had seen enemy armor on the Gabès road. The German force was nothing if not impressive as it moved along the road toward the valley; a large number of Panzers made up the iron heart of the attack, followed by scores of other vehicles including self-propelled artillery, trucks, and armored personnel carriers bearing their loads of *Panzergrenadiere*, some of them alighting to move on foot in the wake of the advancing armor. Initially advancing en masse, the *Kampfgruppe* deployed into three *Angriffsgruppen* as it approached the foothills of the hills that flanked the road. One column, consisting of II./PzGrenRgt 69 supported by Panzers, moved off to the north in the direction of Djebel el Ank; Kradschützen-Bataillon 10 moved off to the southwest, heading for Djebel Berda and the Chott El Guettar; and the remaining force, which included the majority of the Panzers as well as II./PzGrenRgt 86, headed straight for the heart of the American line around Hill 336 and the El Keddab ridge (Schick 2013: 499).

The SdKfz 251 half-tracks of the northern German force arrived at the base of Djebel el Mcheltat (Hill 482 on the American military maps) just as dawn was breaking. Major Paul Pomée, commander of II./PzGrenRgt 69, detailed two companies of *Panzergrenadiere* supported by a handful of Panzers to make for Hill 482's crest. They pushed hard and fast up the hill's lower slopes, but the incline coupled with the appallingly rough nature of the terrain soon made further mechanized progress impossible, forcing the men to alight and scramble up the hillside on foot. Soon enough Germans started falling, hit by accurate rifle fire, but as the American positions were all made from built-up stacks of the loose scree that littered the hill it was very difficult to tell where the rounds were coming from. As the *Panzergrenadiere* came closer they were showered with hand grenades from the slopes above them, throwing their own in retaliation. Even their vehicles came under attack, though they were some way back from the heart of the fight; soldiers on the crest used M1903

A PzKpfw IV Ausf F2 beside an SdKfz 252 ammunition carrier pictured on a winding Tunisian road, 1943. The German Panzer divisions were mostly equipped with the PzKpfw III, but the PzKpfw IV usually accounted for one company in each *Panzer-Abteilung*. The F2 variant mounted the 7.5cm KwK 40 L/43 gun, replacing the short-barreled 7.5cm KwK 37 L/24 close-support gun of earlier models; despite being overly heavy for the chassis that had to support it, the KwK 40 was an effective weapon against Allied armor, and one that was much more common than the 8.8cm guns of schwere Panzer-Abteilung 501. (AirSeaLand Photos)

Grenade fight on Hill 482

The coming of dawn has brought a German attack with it; the main thrust is heading down the Gabès–El Guettar road, but two companies of *Panzergrenadiere* in SdKfz 251s from II./PzGrenRgt 69 (with the support of several Panzers) have broken north with the intention of capturing Djebel el Mcheltat. K/18th Infantry is holding the northern flank of the horseshoe-shaped Hill 482 (as the American military maps designate Djebel el Mcheltat), its 3d Platoon quickly becoming the focal point of the German assault. The ground on which the platoon's squads are located is rocky and unforgiving, most of the men only being able to scrape shallow holes a foot or two deep for protection. As a result, most have built up small walls of loose scree in front of their 'foxholes' to provide some added cover. The *Panzergrenadiere* use their half-tracks to get as far up the slopes as they can, but the steepness of the ascent coupled with the rough terrain forces them to disembark, proceeding on foot to within 50ft of the American position. The fight has developed into a "bombing match," with each side hurling grenades at one another; members of a squad from the 3d Platoon huddle behind their stone sangars, throwing grenade after grenade at the *Panzergrenadiere*. Their sergeant crouches down to avoid being hit, holding his Thompson SMG above the stone "parapet" and firing blind, while an M1903 Springfield-armed rifleman is launching grenades at the half-tracks some 200yd distant. One man, peppered by grenade shrapnel, is being dragged to the rear by the platoon medic.

Springfields to launch rifle grenades, destroying at least three SdKfz 251s and a PzKpfw II light tank.

For their part the defenders of the hill were doing their level best to keep the Germans at arm's length. Captain Clifford B. Raymer's K/18th Infantry had been detailed to occupy the hill during the night, where he had his men dig in and pull together some simple defenses as best they could. Hill 482 was shaped rather like a horseshoe, topped by a thin ridgeline that dominated a 500yd front that would be difficult for any attacker to reach – it was a lot of ground for one company to cover, but its position meant that it could cover any advance along the road 2.5 miles away. Raymer recalled how the half-tracks approached just the way he thought they would, and when the *Panzergrenadiere* were forced to dismount and approach on foot his whole company opened up on them at a range of 200yd (Barron 2017: 101). The toll on the Germans was significant, forcing them to make their way up with care under cover of machine-gun fire from fellow soldiers as well from their half-tracks farther down the slope. Working their way up foot by foot, the *Panzergrenadiere* made it to within 50yd of the crest, but no farther, the whole affair descending into a game of attrition played with bullets and hand grenades that went on for the rest of the morning. In defense of their position the men of K/18th Infantry threw more than 1,300 hand grenades during the course of the morning.

The attack against the American center was carried out by the strongest German units, led by armor from Panzer-Regiment 7 closely followed by the *Panzergrenadiere* of II./PzGrenRgt 86, and was aimed at the section of the 1st Infantry Division's perimeter that was most difficult to defend – the base of the valley. Being more or less flat it provided little good cover for an attacker or defender, with the only significant terrain feature being the El Keddab ridgeline. The linchpin of the ridge (and the American position) was Hill 336, where Colonel Greer had established the command post of the 18th Infantry Regiment. Spread out in trenches and foxholes, the 3/18th Infantry (less Company K, established on Hill 482) was emplaced on the eastern approach to Hill 336.

The German artillery opened up at around 0730hrs, targeting 3/18th Infantry, keeping the US soldiers' heads down as the main assault force approached. The advance was covered by huge smokescreens generated by the Panzers and possibly also supporting artillery, effectively blocking out from view the main body of German armor and their supporting infantry until they were all too close. Captain Sam Carter of D/18th Infantry was dug in on Djebel Berda with a fine view of the developing attack, observing the armored column heading for the 3/18th Infantry positioned by Hill 336; from his vantage point it looked like the battalion was being overrun, with one company's position completely covered by German armor. The Panzers were attempting to kill soldiers who were crouching down low in their foxholes by driving over them and twisting the tank's treads to crush them, the following *Panzergrenadiere* checking the holes at gunpoint for survivors (Kelly 2002: 274). Forced to retreat under the intensity of the Panzer and *Panzergrenadier* attack, the 3/18th Infantry and the nearby 3/16th Infantry scrambled back toward the El Keddab ridge; there, they stopped in a wadi, rallied, and then fought their way forward again, occasionally in merciless hand-to-hand encounters, until they had regained their old positions.

Another spur of the German attack, likely conducted at least in part by Pomée's two remaining companies of II./PzGrenRgt 69, made for the

Men from B/17th FAR near El Guettar prepare their gun to fire, March 23, 1943. They are crewing an obsolescent 155mm M1918 howitzer (the US designation of the French Canon de 155 C modèle 1917 Schneider), the US Army's main medium-caliber artillery piece during World War I. The US Army's medium-artillery batteries were by this time supposed to be equipped with the new 155mm M1 howitzer, but shortages of supply meant that some units, including the one shown here, were still relying on the older guns to provide their supporting fire well into 1943. (Photo12/UIG/Getty Images)

gun line of the 5th (155mm) and 32d (105mm) Field Artillery battalions. Before the intelligence reports had come in informing Allen that a German attack was imminent, he had been in the process of positioning the division in anticipation of launching his own advance. As a result the two artillery battalions had been placed well forward to support the expected progress of the division's infantry. The German advance put the 1st Infantry Division onto a defensive footing, but the 5th and 32d were never repositioned, and now they were exposed. Soon enough the *Panzergrenadiere* were getting uncomfortably close, forcing the American guns – some of which were starting to run out of ammunition – to fire salvoes over open sights at point-blank range, but it was not enough. Spiking the guns with hand grenades, the crews abandoned their weapons and retreated (Atkinson 2002: 440). Each battalion lost six guns.

The M3 GMCs of the 601st Tank Destroyer Battalion were not having an easy time of it either. Though the individual vehicle crews had chosen their positions with care, making the most of whatever cover and concealment was available, many soon found themselves exposed by an old German trick. The approaching Panzers swept the ground in front of them with tracer fire from their coaxial machine guns – when the rounds hit metal they would ricochet off into the air and give away the position of the GMCs, allowing the Panzers to bring their main armament to bear. The lightly armored gun trucks were vulnerable to even medium-caliber artillery or tank fire and several were soon knocked out, but they provided valuable support for the soldiers of the 3/18th Infantry who were bearing the brunt of the attack, and they were also crucial to the defense of the road. The German vanguard was comprised of 22 Panzers of various types, a number of which were pressing along the macadam heading straight for the gap that the road cut through the El Keddab ridge. There was limited room for the Germans to maneuver due to the Chott el Guettar making the ground to the south of the road impenetrable, which helped corral the Panzers and keep them within range of the 601st's 75mm guns. The battalion threw everything it had at the attackers, some of which started running into trouble after a volley from A/601st TDB's guns that forced the Panzers to veer into soft patches of ground, bogging some of them down. In an effort to avoid the 601st's gunnery, other Panzers strayed into a well-placed minefield, the combination of misfortunes suddenly stalling the German advance at around 0820hrs.

The constant (if dwindling) fire from the 601st's guns was augmented by the impressive weight of the US divisional artillery that hammered at the German armored formations. Within the hour the worst of the attack had passed, but the Panzers and their supporting elements had not yet withdrawn and still posed a threat. The 899th Tank Destroyer Battalion, a fresh unit with brand-new M10 GMCs, had been called up to provide support to the 601st; it arrived at around 0950hrs, companies B and C up front with Company A as the reserve. Armed with a 3in gun the M10 packed a punch, but the inexperience of the 899th's crews showed and the lead companies were mauled by their inexperience in dealing with German armored tactics, as well as the accurate gunnery from German armor and antitank guns. The 899th lost seven vehicles for little benefit. All told, the

601st had lost 24 out of its 36 guns, and the day's fighting had some way yet to run.

Kradschützen-Bataillon 10's advance on Djebel Berda proved to be equally unsuccessful, encountering terrain that proved impossible for even its light vehicles to maneuver through. The battalion conducted some probing attacks, but there was no obvious weak point that could aid a rapid exploitation; soon enough, it too had abandoned any attempt on the American position and pulled back toward the cover of Djebel Kreroua, awaiting developments.

As the wave of the German attack receded some crews left the safety of their vehicles to hitch tow ropes to Panzers damaged in the attack toward El Keddab, even though they were still within range of the American guns, a sign of how valuable any potentially salvageable Panzer was. Such courage allowed the crews to rescue several dozen knocked-out Panzers that would hopefully be returned to service by the workshop companies. During the lull after 10. Panzer-Division's failed attack the battle was continued by each side's respective air forces, with both launching sorties against each other's positions. More than one 1st Infantry Division veteran remembered the danger of movement when the Ju 87 Stuka dive-bombers were about, but at least this time the Germans were getting some of their own medicine too. The Americans also used the respite to take stock, evacuate their wounded, and reorganize their defenses.

There was no element of surprise; radio intercepts left no doubt that a second assault was brewing, and it jumped off at 1645hrs. An officer from the 18th Infantry Regiment on Hill 336 watched the German

A group of unidentified American GIs ride along in a Schwerer Panzerspähwagen SdKfz 233 captured from 10. Panzer-Division, presumably around the time of the engagements at El Guettar. The SdKfz 233 was meant to provide fire support to German *Aufklärungs* (reconnaissance) units and was derived from the open-topped SdKfz 263 radio reconnaissance vehicle, but with the substitution of a short-barreled 7.5cm KwK 37 L/24 gun for the radio equipment; the gun was the same model fitted to early PzKpfw IVs and StuG IIIs and mainly used the 7.5cm Sprenggranate 34 high-explosive round, though it could also employ various antiarmor shells such as the Granate 38HL and Panzergranate 39, but their relatively low velocity meant they were of limited value against tanks. (© CORBIS/ Corbis via Getty Images)

attack develop, Panzers rolling forward covered with infantry hitching a ride, many of whom would soon be suffering due to accurate fire from American mortarmen. The German formation was advancing on a similar line to that employed during the morning's main attack, pushing toward the positions of 3/18th Infantry by Hill 336 and the gun line of the 32d Field Artillery Battalion. Darby, sitting with his Rangers on the heights, noted how the German troops moved with deliberation, lurching forward rather than running (Kelly 2002: 275), with the *Panzergrenadiere* moving in the vanguard of the armor, much of which seemed to be hanging back. The leading edge of the German advance was within 1,550yd of the American lines when the storm of American artillery broke over them. Darby watched as salvo after salvo came crashing down dead on target, the detonations blowing great black holes in the ranks of advancing men (Barron 2017: 144). Despite the fury of the shelling the *Panzergrenadiere* pressed onward, seemingly heedless of seeking cover or maneuvering to avoid the worst of the concussive detonations and clouds of shrapnel.

By 1710hrs the attack had reached its zenith, once again pressing in on the positions of the 3/18th Infantry, the German foot soldiers working their way around the position until they had the American battalion encircled. The 3/18th Infantry stayed where it was despite the German attacks, which, poorly supported by armor and suffering increasing numbers of casualties from the artillery bombardment, began to pull back. The earlier resolution the *Panzergrenadiere* had shown in marching through the bombardment could not be sustained. Men began to seek out some shelter from the splinters of metal that filled the air, with large groups of German infantry building up behind dunes and other elements of terrain that hid them from view. Unfortunately for the attackers it was not hard to see which elements of the terrain offered protection, and it took the American gunners very little time to find the reverse slopes of such features. The shells were set to airburst, and caused endless carnage. Brigadier General Clift Andrus, the commander of the 1st Infantry Division's artillery, noted how one particularly large body of men was in just such a predicament, sheltering behind some concealing terrain until the shells began to detonate above their heads, whereupon they broke and started running for the safety of their own lines. Moving in the open the *Panzergrenadiere* were cut to ribbons by shells that were falling in 7yd intervals, Andrus doubting that any of them made it back alive (Atkinson 2002: 443).

By around 1740hrs it was perfectly clear to Broich that to continue pressing the attack would be little better than suicide. Worn out by battering itself against Tunisian hills and American guns, its formations shattered by intense artillery attacks, 10. Panzer-Division pulled back out of range to lick its wounds. Darkness would not see the end of German attacks at El Guettar, which would continue for some days to come. At the Maknassy Pass to the north there had been some German success against Ward's 1st Armored Division, but even that battle saw no American collapse, no wholesale destruction, and no rout. Though 10. Panzer-Division lacked several of its more important assets it was still a powerful combined-arms force with serious weaponry and much experience. The 1st Infantry Division had stopped it dead.

OPPOSITE
The grave of a German soldier who was killed on March 22, 1943. Aside from the veterans of the Deutsches Afrikakorps, many of the German units that had been sent at the end of 1942 to bolster the defense of Tunisia, such as 10. Panzer-Division, effectively ceased to exist at their surrender in May 1943, never being rebuilt, while others, such as the *Kampfgruppen* from Panzer-Division *Hermann Göring*, lost all but a handful of their most experienced officers and men, something that would have serious consequences for that unit's attempt to defend Sicily from Allied invasion a scant two months later. (Eliot Elisofon/The LIFE Picture Collection/Getty Images)

Hauptwachtmeister
Erhard Lege
5./P₃.AR90
8.1.1913   22.3.1943

Analysis

SIDI BOU ZID

The US forces facing the German attack at Sidi Bou Zid were hamstrung by poor planning, strategic misjudgment, and a gross underestimation of Axis capabilities. Several US officers recognized the inadequacy of the US defensive plan even as it was being implemented; forces were too light to fend off a concerted attack, the terrain offered few obstacles or defensible features that would give an attacker pause, and the deployment of armored and infantry units – determined by examining maps rather than the actual environment – left them isolated and unable to support one another.

A US medic helps a wounded half-track gunner swallow a sulfa tablet before treating his wounds during the battle for control of the Sened area, February 1943. The US soldiers who fought at Sidi Bou Zid were mostly new to warfare, some of them undertrained and poorly armed (or even unarmed), and though the 1st Armored Division contingents were well-trained in making effective use of their M4 tanks, they were hamstrung by erroneous doctrine, inexperienced in tank combat, and insufficiently prepared to engage the veterans of 5. Panzerarmee and the DAK. The 1st Armored Division saw two of its combat commands effectively destroyed at Sidi Bou Zid, with the two battalions of the 168th Infantry Regiment hollowed out by casualties and large numbers of men who fell to the Germans as prisoners. (Eliot Elisofon/The LIFE Picture Collection/Getty Images)

For the Germans the plan was tactically sound, though it left many of the larger strategic questions unanswered. Rommel's frustration at the hesitant Axis progress after the initial successes reflected his ambitious outlook, married to a hope that rapid exploitation could retain the initiative and exploit the perceived American weaknesses of inexperience and poor leadership. The German *Kampfgruppen* had the advantage of being drawn from two highly experienced armored units, both of which were supplied with very powerful assets (such as 8.8cm antiaircraft guns and a company of PzKpfw VI Tiger tanks) that they knew how to utilize for best effect.

The failure of the *Kampfgruppen* to deal with the American positions on Djebel Lessouda, Djebel Ksaira, and Djebel Garet Hadid was understandable: the rough ground made the heights relatively safe from armored attack, and the German forces lacked sufficient infantry to divert any to secure the hills. The usual German armored doctrine would have involved throwing a security cordon around isolated enemy strongpoints and then moving on, the cordon awaiting the arrival of a second line of supporting infantry whose role was to mop up just such bypassed positions; the forces of 10. and 21. Panzer-Divisionen lacked the men to perform either function effectively. Fortunately for the Germans, Djebel Lessouda and Djebel Ksaira were too far away to provide any sort of mutual support; the Americans were dreadfully exposed to artillery, air, and infantry assault, their positions being unsuited to serious defense and the troops holding them lacking the supplies and weaponry required. These shortcomings were compounded by the armored debacle on the plain that ensured that for the US soldiers on the hills there would be no help coming any time soon. The American decision to abandon the positions and attempt a breakout was logical, but it came far too late.

A pair of PzKpfw III medium tanks (likely from either 15. or 21. Panzer-Divisionen) with tank riders maneuver along a country road between Tunis and the Algerian border, 1943. Although it was still an important weapon for the German armored units in Tunisia, by early 1943 the PzKpfw III was verging on obsolescence, with even the more recent Ausf J models shown here (that were still fitted with the short-barreled 5cm KwK 38 L/42 gun) proving inadequate against some of the more heavily armed and armored Allied tanks, not to mention the newly arrived American M4 medium tank. (Bundesarchiv Bild 101I-788-0006-16 Foto: Dullin)

THE KASSERINE PASS

OPPOSITE

Artillery was the strongest and best-trained arm of US forces in Tunisia, and though its full effects were often muted due to poor tactical deployment and a lack of coordination with the infantry and armored units that it was supporting, it could be very effective when used well, as many German formations found to their cost. The guns were excellent, and they were served by well-trained crews led by competent officers. With well-thought-through positioning, good forward observation, and a reliable supply of ammunition, such weapons could and did make a significant contribution to the defeat of the 10. Panzer-Division *Kampfgruppe* at El Guettar. Here, a T19 HMC gun crew are depicted in the process of firing their 105mm M2A1 howitzer toward German and Italian positions during battles around Sened, February 1, 1943. The vehicle's secondary armament, a .50-caliber Browning M2 HMG, can also be seen clearly. During the assault of 10. Panzer-Division at El Guettar the cannon companies of both the 16th and 18th Infantry regiments saw action in repulsing the initial attacks and in the subsequent days of fighting. Each one of a division's infantry regiments contained a cannon company which provided close artillery support; cannon companies usually had six 75mm T30 HMCs (which like the T19 were built on the M3 half-track chassis but armed with 75mm "pack" howitzers) and two 105mm T19s. (Eliot Elisofon/The LIFE Picture Collection/Getty Images)

The decision to send 1,200 green engineers to establish a defensive position at Kasserine was remarkable for all the wrong reasons. The addition of Kelleher's infantry with its artillery support was an obvious requirement but still fell far short of what was needed. The US deployment at the pass failed to make the most of the defensive tools available (the mines), and the decision to place most of the infantry and engineers on the valley floor and to hold the pass shoulders with only two (later four) platoons was a potential invitation to disaster. Surrounding units were enmeshed in complex and overlapping chains of command, making it harder for the Allied forces to respond effectively to a serious attack upon the pass.

The engineers' performance should not be judged too harshly. Lacking proper infantry training and combat experience, they faced German veterans aggressively supported by armor and artillery. With no immediate prospect of relief or reinforcement, the engineers saw most of their tank destroyers knocked out, and the majority of their artillery withdrew when the going got too hot; that only some of them ran is remarkable. The men of the 1/26th Infantry, in the same situation, fought as well as could be expected. For the US forces at Kasserine most of the big mistakes – the paltry allocation of forces, poor command and control with other units and commands, and inadequate support – were made before they even reached the pass.

The Germans' initial attempt to punch through Kasserine with a single thrust from a reconnaissance unit suggests that they were confident that the Americans were still brittle from their rough handling at Sidi Bou Zid and Sbeïtla. That rebuff led to the commitment of Panzergrenadier-Regiment *Afrika*, and although both of that unit's battalions made some progress on each side of the pass, neither managed to breach Stark's line on the first day. Kampfgruppe *DAK* had a decent allotment of artillery – nine batteries, including *Nebelwerfern* – but visibility was poor and there were no German forward observers on the heights to direct their fire. Sorties by the Luftwaffe were also lacking, meaning that most of the German infantry's direct support came from the guns of Panzer-Regiment 5. The bulk of the fighting fell to the two *Panzergrenadier* battalions, outnumbered by the defending Americans. Bülowius's *Kampfgruppe* did not have enough infantry to force the issue.

If Rommel had concentrated his assets on Kasserine he would certainly have broken through within the first day. If he had maintained that concentration rather than advancing on three divergent axes he would still have found himself driving into a hornets' nest with ever-diminishing fuel, ammunition, and manpower. Even if his audacity was matched by luck, it would still have been a most unlikely German victory.

EL GUETTAR

Conducting no reconnaissance, 10. Panzer-Division seemed surprised by the rough terrain it encountered when trying to assault the hills at El Guettar, and was unable to neutralize the American artillery. With 10. Panzer-Division fielding only two battalions of *Panzergrenadiere* and two companies of

Kradschützen, it was wildly optimistic to think that the Germans had enough infantry to mount three separate concurrent attacks, mostly over ground impassable for vehicles. The fact that such attacks were conducted against an infantry division at full strength deployed in depth and with significant supporting assets suggests that the Germans seriously underestimated the enemy they were engaging.

The fate of the 5th and 32d Field Artillery battalions notwithstanding, the value of the American artillery was demonstrated clearly. Air power also began to make a real difference, with additional Allied airfields denying the Luftwaffe the one-sided superiority it had enjoyed for so long. Though the Americans lacked tank support, their rather vulnerable M3 GMCs and new M10 GMCs brought them a much-needed antitank capability, especially against a force equipped with PzKpfw III and PzKpfw IV medium tanks that lacked the long-range destructive punch of the Tigers. The tank-destroyer battalions employed at El Guettar made a material difference to the battle's outcome.

Patton's aggressive leadership was important in turning around American fortunes in North Africa, as was the fact that by mid-March II Corps was on the move, taking the fight to the enemy. The reorganization of lines of command, the reassembly of the divisions, and the concentration of national forces within their own clearly delineated zones of operation all went a considerable way to undoing some of the tangled mess that had mired American effectiveness in the first months of 1943. El Guettar demonstrated that the base metal of American forces was sound; poor strategies and careless handling had exacted a high cost, but when those deficiencies were rectified the essential strength of the US Army began to show through.

Aftermath

Of all the American senior commanders, Lloyd Fredendall has emerged from the Tunisian campaign almost entirely devoid of credit. His abrasive personal style resulted in poor relationships with several of his key officers, including Orlando Ward of the 1st Armored Division; he certainly did not lead from the front – forgivable in victory, not so much in defeat – and his deployment of II Corps assets down to battalion level evinced a mistrust of subordinates and an unrealistic sense of his own capabilities

An abandoned M3 half-track that has enjoyed a brief life in German service. Constant failures of supply coupled with the grinding attrition of war meant that German formations were always short of vehicles, the DAK in particular having to make up such shortfalls by pressing *Beute-Fahrzeug* (literally "booty vehicles," captured Allied trucks, cars, and such like) into use on a consistent and widespread basis. *Panzergrenadier* units, always short of their own armored personnel carriers, leapt at the opportunity to utilize vehicles such as the M3. (AirSeaLand Photos)

that would cost his men dearly. His replacement, George Patton, gifted with competence allied with aggression, was a notable improvement. Of the divisional commanders, Ward was capable but diffident, lacking aggression and hopelessly compromised by his poor relationships with Fredendall and later Patton, his weak field command being shown up by his division's rough handling at Sidi Bou Zid and later Maknassy. Relieved by Patton soon after being wounded at El Guettar, he served in training posts until returning to Europe at the head of the 20th Armored Division in the closing months of the war. Both the 1st Infantry Division's Terry Allen and the 34th Infantry Division's Charles Ryder proved capable and popular with their men, whose reputations rose as their divisions reassembled themselves and fought as coherent units during the later stages of the Tunisian campaign. Allen's idiosyncrasies would see him moved from the 1st Armored Division during the Sicilian campaign, but he returned to the war at the head of the 104th Infantry Division, while Ryder was promoted to the command of IX Corps in 1944.

Erwin Rommel, who had made such a name for himself in the Western Desert, proved unable to sustain his star in Tunisia for a host of reasons, not least among them a rivalry with Hans-Jürgen von Arnim that reflected poorly on both men. Saved from the end in North Africa, Rommel would play an important role in preparing and fighting the German defenses in Normandy, though his associations with the July 20 bomb plotters would result in his suicide on October 14, 1944. Arnim, succeeding Rommel to the

An American patrol moves toward a ridgeline. The failures of American arms at Sidi Bou Zid and Kasserine led Rommel and many other Germans to see the US forces opposing them as generally poor soldiers who were badly organized and led. There was some truth to those assumptions, but German successes had to be seen in the context of their greater experience as well as the teething problems that any new army was likely to face when coming fresh to war. The reorganization undertaken by Patton had shown that the US infantry could be every bit as potent an enemy for the Axis as the Commonwealth forces they had been battling for the past three years. (Eliot Elisofon/The LIFE Picture Collection/Getty Images)

German

Panzer-Divisionen were rather diverse units, with few of them enjoying exactly the same organization due to quirks inherited from their establishment coupled with ongoing operational adaptations. With that caveat, a standard *Panzer-Division* in 1942–43 would comprise one *Panzer-Regiment* (two or three *Panzer-Abteilungen*, each one with a *Stabs-Kompanie*, two or three PzKpfw III-equipped *Panzer-Kompanien*, one PzKpfw IV-equipped *Panzer-Kompanie*, and a *Panzer-Werkstatt-Kompanie*); two *Panzergrenadier-Regimenter*, a *Panzer-Aufklärungs-Abteilung*; a *Panzerjäger-Abteilung*; a *Panzer-Pionier-Bataillon*; a *Panzer-Artillerie-Regiment* (consisting of three *Feldartillerie-Abteilungen* and one *Flak-Abteilung*); and a *Panzer-Nachrichten-Abteilung*. A *Panzergrenadier-Regiment* comprised a *Stabs-Kompanie*, two battalions (I. Bataillon having three *Infanterie-Kompanien* and one *sMG-Kompanie* numbered 1. to 4.; the same for II. Bataillon, but numbered 5. to 8.), an *Infanteriegeschütz-Kompanie* (9. Kompanie), and a *leichte Flak-Kompanie* (10. Kompanie).

10. Panzer-Division consisted of Panzer-Regiment 7, Panzergrenadier-Regimenter 69 and 86, Panzer-Artillerie-Regiment 90, Panzer-Aufklärungs-Abteilung 10, Kradschützen-Bataillon 10, Panzerjäger-Abteilung 90, Panzer-Pionier-Bataillon 49, Panzer-Nachrichten-Abteilung 90, Panzer-Versorgungstruppen 90, and Heeres-Flak-Artillerie-Abteilung 302. When at full strength Panzer-Regiment 7 had a total of 143 tanks (129 combat tanks, 14 command tanks); it had two *Abteilungen*, both with a *Stabs-Kompanie* (three PzKpfw III), three *leichte Panzerkompanien* (16 PzKpfw III each), and one *mittlerer Panzerkompanie* (12 PzKpfw IV). In the build-up to the attack on Sidi Bou Zid, 10. Panzer-Division had around 140 combat-ready tanks: 20 PzKpfw II, 100 PzKpfw III, and 20 PzKpfw IV. This establishment was further bolstered by the addition of one company of Tigers from schwere Panzer-Abteilung 501, attached to the division from February 8, 1943. On February 26, the Tiger company was redesignated III./PzRgt 7 and reinforced with 15 PzKpfw IV tanks; heavy losses would see the remnants of the *Abteilung* absorbed by the newly arrived schwere Panzer-Abteilung 504 on March 17, 1943. Kradschützen-Bataillon 10 had five companies: 1. Kompanie (SdKfz 223 and 222 armored cars), 2. Kompanie (*Schützen*, "armored infantry," in SdKfz 250 half-tracks); 3. and 4. Kompanien (*Kradschützentruppe*,

"motorcycle infantry"), and 5. Kompanie (*Pionier-Zug*, *Panzerjäger-Zug* with 5cm PaK 38 antitank guns, and two *Infanteriegeschütz-Züge*).

21. Panzer-Division consisted of Panzer-Regiment 5 (two battalions in February 1943, with I. Bataillon being a consolidation of I. and II. Bataillone, with II. Bataillon being formed from the newly transferred Panzer-Abteilung 190 from 90. leichte Afrika-Division), Panzergrenadier-Regimenter 47 and 104, Aufklärungs-Abteilung (mot.) 3, Panzer-Artillerie-Regiment 155, Panzerjäger-Abteilung 200, Panzer-Pionier-Bataillon 220, Panzer-Versorgungstruppen 200, and Heeres-Flakartillerie-Abteilung 305.

90. leichte Afrika-Division consisted of Panzer-Abteilung 190 (until its transfer to 21. Panzer-Division), Panzergrenadier-Regimenter 155, 200, and 361, Panzergrenadier-Regiment *Afrika*, Artillerie-Regiment 190, Panzerjäger-Abteilung 190, Aufklärungs-Abteilung 580, Pionier-Bataillon 900, Panzer-Nachrichten-Abteilung 190, and Divisions-Nachschubführer 190.

An American infantryman holding a captured MP 40 submachine gun, near El Guettar, Tunisia. The differences between the MP 40 and its earlier incarnation, the MP 38, were not readily noticeable on casual inspection, the main changes occurring in the methods of manufacture to make for a more quickly produced and affordable weapon by moving away from a milled receiver to one made out of stamped metal. The rest bar on the underside of the barrel was designed to allow troops firing from vehicles or armored personnel carriers to hook the muzzle of their weapon over the lip of the vehicle's side, ensuring that recoil or the passage over rough ground did not result in the gun firing into the inside wall of the carrier, leading to potentially deadly ricochets. (Eliot Elisofon/The LIFE Picture Collection/Getty Images)

BIBLIOGRAPHY

Atkinson, Rick (2002). *An Army at Dawn. The War in North Africa, 1942–1943.* New York, NY: Henry Holt.

Barron, Leo (2017). *Patton's First Victory: How General George Patton Turned the Tide in North Africa and Defeated the Afrika Korps at El Guettar.* Guilford, CT: Stackpole.

Barry, Steven Thomas (2011). "Battle-scarred and Dirty: US Army Tactical Leadership in the Mediterranean Theater, 1942–1943." Columbus, OH: Ohio State University. Available online at: https://etd.ohiolink.edu/!etd.send_file?accession=osu1313541748&disposition=inline

Bedell, A.D., et al. (1984). *Battle Analysis of the Battle of Sidi Bou Zid, Tunisia, North Africa. Defensive, Encircled Forces, 14 February 1943.* Fort Leavenworth, KS: Army Command and General Staff College, Combat Studies Institute. Available online at: http://www.dtic.mil/dtic/tr/fulltext/u2/a151626.pdf

Blumenson, Martin (1967). *Kasserine Pass. Rommel's Bloody Climactic Battle for Tunisia.* Boston, MA: Houghton Mifflin.

Butler, Allen S. (1949). *The Operations of the First Infantry Division at El Guettar, 20–30 March, Tunisian Campaign.* Fort Benning, GA: The Infantry School.

Calhoun, Mark T. (2003). *Defeat at Kasserine: American Armor Doctrine, Training, and Battle Command in Northwest Africa, World War II.* Fort Leavenworth, KS: USACGSSC. Available online at: http://cgsc.cdmhost.com/cdm/singleitem/collection/p4013coll2/id/31/rec/3

Drake, Thomas D. (1945). *Operations of the 168th Infantry between the dates of 24 December 1942 and 17 February 1943.* San Francisco, CA: IX Corps Headquarters, US Army. Available online at: http://www.34infdiv.org/history/168inf/4212-4303DrakeRpt.pdf

FM 23-15 (1940). Browning Automatic Rifle, Caliber .30, M1918A2 with Bipod.

FM 100-5 (1941). Field Service Regulations: Operations.

Hackett, Paul T. (1950). *The Operations of the 1st Infantry Division at El Guettar, 20–24 March 1943 (Tunisian Campaign).* Fort Benning, GA: The Infantry School. Available online at: http://www.benning.army.mil/library/content/Virtual/Donovanpapers/wwii/STUP2/HackettPaulT%201LT.pdf

Hartmann, Bernd (2011). *Panzers in the Sand: The History of the Panzer-Regiment 5, Vol. 2: 1942–45.* Barnsley: Pen & Sword Military.

Hougen, John H. (1949). *The Story of the Famous 34th Infantry Division.* Arlington, VA: Self-published.

Howe, George F. (1957). *Northwest Africa: Seizing the Initiative in the West.* Washington, DC: Center of Military History, US Army.

Jentz, Thomas L. (2001). *Dreaded Threat. The 8.8 cm Flak 18/36/37 in the Anti-Tank Role.* (Panzer Tracts). Boyds, MD: Panzer Tracts.

Kasserine Pass Battles (1993). *Kasserine Pass Battles: Staff Ride Background Materials.* US Army CMH. Available online at: http://www.history.army.mil/books/Staff-Rides/kasserine/kasserine.htm

Kelly, Orr (2002). *Meeting the Fox: The Allied Invasion of Africa, from Operation Torch to Kasserine Pass to Victory in Tunisia.* New York, NY: John Wiley & Sons.

Knickerbocker, Hubert R., et al. (1980). *Danger Forward: The Story of the First Division in World War II.* Nashville, TN: Battery Press. First published 1947.

Luck, Hans von (2002). *Panzer Commander: The Memoirs of Colonel Hans von Luck.* London: Cassell.

Mansoor, Peter (1999). *The GI Offensive in Europe: The Triumph of American Infantry Divisions, 1941–1945.* Lawrence, KS: University Press of Kansas.

Pyle, Ernie, ed. David Nichols (1986). *Ernie's War: The Best of Ernie Pyle's World War II Dispatches.* New York, NY: Random House.

Rolf, David (2001). *The Bloody Road to Tunis: Destruction of the Axis Forces in North Africa, November 1942–May 1943.* London: Greenhill.

Rottman, Gordon M. (2008). *M3 Medium Tank vs Panzer III: Kasserine Pass 1943.* Duel 10. Oxford: Osprey.

Sayen, John J. (2006). *US Army Infantry Divisions 1942–43.* Battle Orders 17. Oxford: Osprey.

Schick, Albert (2013). *Combat History of the 10. Panzer Division, 1939–1943.* Winnipeg: J.J. Fedorowicz.

US Army Historical Division (1989). *To Bizerte with the II Corps.* War Department, 1943.

Wheeler, James Scott (2007). *The Big Red One: America's Legendary 1st Infantry Division from World War I to Desert Storm.* Lawrence, KS: University Press of Kansas.

Zaloga, Steven J. (2005). *Kasserine Pass 1943: Rommel's last victory.* Campaign 152. Oxford: Osprey.

INDEX

References to illustrations are shown in **bold**.